EUROPE REINVENTED

How COVID-19 Is Changing the European Union

Peter Van Kemseke

EUROPE REINVENTED

How COVID-19 Is Changing the European Union

Boeklyn

*To all true and truly European leaders,
current and future.*

Europe Reinvented. How COVID-19 Is Changing the European Union
© 2020 Peter Van Kemseke / Boeklyn International (Belgium)

www.boeklyn.com/international
info@boeklyn.com

Copy editing by Heather Sills
Book design by Palabras

DISCLAIMER:
The views and opinions expressed in this book are those of the author.

ISBN 9789463882750
NUR 697
D/2020/14735/03

Table of contents

PART 1

AN INFECTED UNION, A CRUMBLING UNITY

CHAPTER 1

Going Viral

- Why China was happy with the name COVID-19
- How the World Health Organization reacted to the outbreak
- How the novel coronavirus affected US-Chinese relations

'A MORE PROSPEROUS AND GREENER YEAR'

Airports are fascinating. They are living organisms. Gateways for people, goods, lifestyles and ideas from and to all corners of the world. I love them, and I usually don't mind having to spend just a bit more time in the departures hall when my flight is delayed. There is never a dull moment in an airport.

When the words 'delayed/retrasado' flashed up on the screen, I knew I would be spending my final hours of 2019 at Barajas-Madrid International Airport. That night, it was hard to imagine that this was the fifth busiest airport in Europe, serving almost 58 million passengers a year. By the early evening, the departures hall in Terminal 1 was almost empty. It was New Year's Eve; shops, bars and restaurants were closing earlier than usual. It was a strange feeling. Nobody could have predicted that just a couple of months later, such emptiness would for several weeks become the new norm in many European airports. With time to kill, I went through the tweets of the day. 'I wish you all the best for 2020, a more prosperous and greener year built on even greater trust #Europe', president of the European Council Charles Michel had posted earlier in the day. Greater trust was indeed something to wish for. Despite all the optimism that seems to be a moral duty for politicians, many observers expected (another) difficult year ahead for the European Union.

I had spent the past few days going through a wide range of foresight reports. Foresight means scanning the horizon for emerging trends in international politics. For a brief moment, it puts aside the issues of the day and looks to the future. My interest in this was triggered during a meeting I had, just before the Christmas break, with European Commission vice-president Maroš Šefčovič, in charge of – amongst other things – 'Strategic Foresight'. It was the first time that foresight was included in the job description of a commissioner. If we manage to understand the megatrends that will determine international relations in the coming decades, we will be in a position to better shape them, or so the reasoning goes.

The headlines of that final day of 2019 lived up surprisingly well to some of the trends predicted in the foresight reports of major private consultancy firms and international organisations alike. After pro-Iranian protesters had stormed the US embassy in Iraq, president Trump sent strong warnings to Iran: 'If it comes to a conflict', he said, 'Iran wouldn't last long.' In Afghanistan, the Taliban continued its attacks against security forces, killing more than twenty troops. In Libya, the Associated Press reported, huge sums of European money had been diverted to intertwined networks of militiamen, traffickers and coast guard members who exploited migrants, apparently with full knowledge of some UN officials.

Further East, North Korean leader Kim Jong-un announced that he would continue to build up its nuclear arsenal, while devastating floods in the Indonesian capital of Jakarta, a deadly typhoon in the Philippines and horrific bushfires in Australia illustrated why climate change and natural disasters would continue to top the list of megatrends. An op-ed in the Spanish newspaper *El Pais* argued that 2020 would be 'the year of climate justice', while in *Le Monde*, an opinion-maker focused on how algorithms and new technologies would impact our way of life. In neighbouring Italy, the leader of the right-wing Lega party promised his comeback in 2020, reminding Europeans – on the off-chance they had forgotten – that populism was a political force to be reckoned with. And just before boarding, I noticed on the site of a German newspaper that chancellor Merkel intended to use the German 2020 EU presidency 'to ensure a stronger role of Europe in the world.' Geopolitics, migration, climate change, the fight against populism... European leaders certainly had a busy year ahead.

MEANWHILE IN CHINA...

That evening, Chinese president Xi Jinping gave his annual New Year's speech to the nation. His message was one of self-confidence. 'Everything is flourishing across our motherland', he said. Evidence to support that claim was easy to find. At the start of this year, and for the first time in history – not just in Chinese history but in human history – Planet Earth had visited the far side of the moon, thanks to a Chinese lunar probe. China was close to finishing its own navigation satellite system, an alternative to the American GPS and the European Galileo systems, and would soon have its first self-developed aircraft carrier. On top of that, in the autumn, China's women's national volleyball team had won the World Cup.

Whether it was in technological power, military power or in public relations, China was doing just fine. All thanks to the many people who had worked tirelessly right until the very last moments of the year. 'Your hard work is greatly appreciated', were the president's final words.

Amongst those people still at work that day were health department officials in the Chinese city of Wuhan. On 31 December, they informed the World Health Organization that 27 cases of pneumonia had been detected in their city. According to the People's Daily, the official newspaper of the Communist Party of China, there were some similarities with the SARS virus, the 'Severe Acute Respiratory Syndrome' that had killed hundreds of people worldwide some fifteen years earlier. The international media were not paying too much attention to this news. When they did, it usually amounted to an article filed away under 'medical news', rehashing the information published by the Chinese party paper.

At that point, very little was known about this viral pneumonia, at least publicly. But in Wuhan's medical circles, there was concern. For some time already. In the second week of December 2019, a small number of patients had shown up in local hospitals with symptoms very similar to the flu. They were coughing, had fever, and had problems breathing. Some were sent back home or back to work. When patients began pouring in and the usual treatment did not seem to be working, doctors started to delve deeper into these cases. They soon found out that several of them – around two thirds of the first group of patients – had a link to a local wet market: the Huanan Seafood Wholesale Market.

Wet markets are very common in China and the rest of Asia. Anyone who has visited Indonesia, Vietnam or Hong Kong has probably been to one. The aroma – some would call it smell – of freshness is simply unforgettable.

Wet markets are popular places where you can buy a wide variety of affordable food, from meat and fish to vegetables and fruits, all laid out on display in the open air. As a traditional, short-chain form of food retail, they face increasing competition from supermarkets and convenience stores. These larger businesses are plugged into the global food chain, offering processed food to Asia's expanding middle class. For millions of local farmers, who keep their products fresh by regularly pouring water on them (hence 'wet' market), these places are their main source of income and often their main way of keeping afloat. In most wet markets selling live animals is a thing of the past. An exception is fish-on-ice, very much like a fish market in many European countries. Live poultry is generally forbidden since the outbreak of avian flu in the late 1990s.

The Huanan Seafood Wholesale Market, however, was different. At this huge 50,000 square metre market, several of the more than 1000 traders sold more than apples and chicken meat. Laid out on wooden tables along the narrow, over-crowded lanes in the western part of the market, wild animals were being sold. Even exotic ones like bats, snakes, lizards or baby crocodiles. In all shapes and sizes. Dead or alive.

Some of the first patients who were admitted to Wuhan's hospitals had worked there or at least visited the market just before they fell ill. Two of them were treated by Dr. Ai Fen, the director of the A&E department at Wuhan Central Hospital. On 30 December, she got lab results back for one of her patients: 'SARS Coronavirus'. She knew immediately what to do: sound the alarm. She circled the word SARS, took a picture and sent it to some colleagues. From there, it ended up in the hands of a young ophthalmologist, Li Wenliang, who posted it in a WeChat group of former classmates.

The news spread like wildfire. Before long, Li himself,

just like Dr. Ai and seven other whistleblowers, would be severely reprimanded by the hospital and the city of Wuhan for 'spreading rumours'. Online social media posts about the virus were deleted, and the journalists who posted them faced pressure from local authorities. For 34-year-old Li, there was an even more dramatic turn of events. He was infected with the virus and died in the line of duty in early February 2020.

MEET THE CORONA FAMILY

The moment Dr. Ai got those first test results, Chinese doctors knew the enemy they were fighting. Or at least they knew the family to which that enemy belonged: the corona family, named after the 'crown' ('corona' in Latin) created by the spiky proteins that surround the actual virus particle, just like the thorns of a crown. Coronaviruses usually circulate in animals. Some species get sick. Others, like bats, have – over time – become immune, which makes them the perfect hosts. Not only to coronaviruses, but also to other viruses, such as Ebola, Nipah or Hendra.
Six of these coronaviruses have managed to expand their territory to humans. Four of them were rather harmless, albeit annoying, comparable to a common cold. Two others, however, turned out to be much more dangerous for humans. In the mid-1990s, one strain jumped from bats to camels. In the early 2010s, it then jumped to humans, initially in Saudi Arabia and Qatar, causing the so-called MERS epidemics (Middle East respiratory syndrome). A decade earlier, in China, a new coronavirus had found its way from a bat population to a group of masked palm civets that were sold in an animal market in the city of Guangdong. From this cat-like creature it jumped to humans which caused the 2002-2003 SARS-CoV epidemics. Some 800 infected people were killed globally.

This new 2019 virus was the seventh coronavirus to infect humans. It probably jumped from an animal to a human being some time between early October and early December, and then existed in a latent phase for several weeks. As soon as the newcomer was detected, the next question was: how did it fit into the corona family? Scientists soon discovered that it was a cousin of SARS-CoV, given its 79% similarity in genetic make-up. That answered a few questions, but not all. Was it as lethal as SARS, which had killed around 10% of those infected? Could it be transmitted between people or only between animals and humans? And how contagious was it exactly? These questions remained unanswered when *The New York Times* published its very first news article on the virus, on 6 January 2020, soon after the Chinese had notified the WHO and the US of their pneumonia cases. The next day, *The Wall Street Journal* revealed: 'New Virus Discovered by Chinese Scientists'. Meanwhile back in China, the authorities tried to reassure the world: 'it is controllable, preventable, curable'.

COVID-19: WHAT'S IN A NAME?

Now that the family issue was settled, the new coronavirus, as it was initially referred to, was due a proper name. Given its genetic structure, scientists of the International Committee on Taxonomy of Viruses baptised it: 'severe acute respiratory syndrome coronavirus 2 (SARS-CoV-2)'. Then the World Health Organization had to choose the name of the disease it caused. It settled for the neutral name 'Corona Virus Disease 2019' (COVID-19).

I have always been intrigued by name-giving, especially when it comes to catastrophic events. Names are never innocent. Take hurricanes. In the late 1970s the World Meteorological Organization (WMO) decided to stop giving only female names to hurricanes after decade-long pressure from feminist groups and enlightened politicians. In 2001, the WMO was forced to withdraw the name 'Israel' from the list of names for upcoming storms, after huge protests led by the newspaper *The Jerusalem Post*. It was replaced by 'Ivo'. (Incidentally, the name Adolph was allowed to stick around). And in 2014, Malaysia asked for the name Sonamu to be taken off the list of future storms because it sounded too much like 'tsunami'. Best avoided! The World Health Organization was fully aware of such considerations when it decided on the name for the new disease: 'We had to find a name that did not refer to a geographical location, an animal, an individual or group of people, and which is also pronounceable and related to the disease', it explained in a tweet. Communication was important. That's also why in its public messaging, the WHO generally refers to the COVID-19 virus, and not to the SARS-CoV-2 virus. The name SARS alone could cause panic, especially in those countries that had been severely affected by the SARS epidemic in 2002-2003.

The way the World Health Organization labelled the disease and referred to the virus was without doubt welcomed in Beijing. Even though the outbreak of the virus had undeniably started in China, and even though China was – then – still the epicentre, this was not reflected in the name. Unlike previous pandemics such as the Asian flu, the Mexican flu or – much earlier – the Spanish flu. Beijing had many other reasons to welcome the WHO approach in the early weeks of the epidemic. The organisation's public messages very much echoed those of the Chinese authorities. In mid-January China still argued that there was no clear evidence of human-to-human transmission of the virus. The WHO repeated that information, even though at that point several medical staff working in Wuhan's hospitals had been infected by their patients. It also used and published the number of cases directly as the Chinese sent them, even though many experts assumed that the real numbers were much higher. The WHO did not have much choice. It wasn't until mid-February that a WHO team of experts was allowed to visit China, after a meeting between the director-general and president Xi Jinping in Beijing in late January. At least until then, the WHO depended exclusively on the official information it got from China.

China's relationship with the World Health Organization is a complex one. China's voluntary contribution to the WHO is around \$11 million a year, a fraction of the organisation's total budget, or even of the US contribution, worth \$400 million. But in the wider UN system, China's influence is rising. From my diplomatic posting to the UN in New York, some fifteen years ago, I remember

China as a very important but predominantly defensive player. China intervened, usually by hitting the brakes, when its national interest was directly at stake. Since then, Beijing has clearly developed a more offensive agenda, in line with its global, multilateral ambitions. Today, it is the second-largest contributor to the UN peacekeeping budget and it will soon be the second most important contributor to the regular UN budget, rising above 10%. That buys them more engagement, more visibility, and more authority throughout the UN system.

But even if you take all this into consideration, the praise the WHO leadership reserved for the way in which China handled the outbreak of the epidemic was remarkable. After his meeting with the Chinese president Xi Jinping, the Ethiopian WHO director general Tedros Adhanom Ghebreyesus hailed 'the commitment from the top leadership, and the transparency they had demonstrated'. When a couple of days later the WHO declared the coronavirus a global health emergency (the sixth one in ten years!), he praised the 'extraordinary measures' the Chinese authorities had taken. There was no reason to limit trade or travel to China, the WHO even opposed it. (Meanwhile, on the same day, the US warned Americans not to travel to China.) Declaring the epidemic a global health emergency should not be considered a vote of no confidence in China, the WHO stressed. And in their report, the WHO experts who had visited China had nothing but praise for China's 'bold approach to contain the rapid spread' of the virus. 'China had rolled out perhaps the most ambitious, agile and aggressive disease containment effort in history', the report continued.

THE TOXIC US-CHINESE RELATIONSHIP

How could so much eulogy not have irritated the US, and even more so its president? Trump's reaction was easy to predict. His entire first term was dominated by a confrontation with China. Both countries engaged in a trade war, with the US imposing tariffs on Chinese goods worth more than $360 billion, and China retaliating for more than $110 billion. China's ambitious Belt and Road Initiative, its projection of (military) power in its neighbourhood, its strong interest in international organisations, including the WHO, the role of companies like Huawei in the roll-out of the 5G network... all thorns in the side of the US president. Before long, the COVID-19 epidemic too got embroiled in this broader big power rivalry.

As soon as the first infected person on American soil was confirmed – a 35-year-old man who had returned to Washington State after visiting family in Wuhan – the virus was framed as a foreign threat. In an interview by CNBC on 22 January, against the backdrop of the World Economic Forum in Davos, president Trump stated: 'It's one person coming in from China, we have it under control.' In later statements, he repeatedly called it a 'Chinese virus' ('It comes from China, no?'), ignoring the WHO's advice not to link the virus to a particular region. In the last two weeks of March, Trump referred no fewer than twenty times to the 'China virus'. US secretary of state Mike Pompeo went even further. When his colleagues at the Foreign Ministers meeting of the G7 – the seven leading industrialised democracies – refused to explicitly refer to the 'Wuhan virus' in the final agreement, he simply stopped the text going out.

Throughout the crisis, accusations about who was responsible for the outbreak and where it started went back and forth between the two rival nations. In mid-March, a spokesman for the Chinese Foreign Ministry perpetuated a theory that American soldiers who had visited the Military World Games in Wuhan the previous October had introduced the virus in China. His tweets got 160 million views, and were retweeted by official media as well as by many – though not all – Chinese ambassadors. Shortly before, Republican senator Tom Cotton had suggested, on Fox News, that the virus actually had its origins in a biochemical lab in Wuhan and was accidentally released. Exactly the scenario depicted by the 1981 fictional novel The Eyes of Darkness, in which the author, Dean Koontz, wrote about the virus Wuhan-400 that was developed in a Chinese military laboratory in the Wuhan region.

Fiction or not, this scenario was at one point or another also raised by the US secretary of defense, the secretary of state and the president himself. In that case, the Huanan Seafood Wholesale Market, which according to foreign secretary Pompeo was 'just a handful of miles away' from the Wuhan Institute of Virology, was not the place where the virus originated from, but where it spread from. Scientists and US top defence officials are sceptical. But the story nevertheless dominated a large part of the news.

In this (dis)information war it was the journalists who were caught in the crossfire. In mid-March Beijing expelled thirteen journalists from three major US newspapers in retaliation to Chinese journalists being put under closer scrutiny in the US. Spokesperson for the foreign ministry, Geng Shuang, asked the US to stop its 'cold war mentality'. The New York Times also called China's crackdown against journalists 'an unfortunate echo of the Cold War'. The stakes for both China and the US were high. China wanted to downplay its role in the global outbreak and shift the focus away from the missteps made by withholding information, often at a local level, in the very first weeks.

But China also had an offensive agenda. Once the worst was over and the economy even began to bounce back, China was keen to show that the Chinese model for handling such a crisis was far superior to the western, democratic model. Even some of my most progressive and liberal friends admired the fact that the Chinese were able to build a brand-new hospital in Wuhan in about a week. The desire to be recognised as a country that dealt with the crisis in an 'effective, unprecedented and transparent', even heroic, way was obvious in most of the public messaging of the Chinese authorities, both inside and outside China.

At the same time, they wanted to turn the crisis into a geopolitical opportunity, and promote the image of China as a responsible major power, perhaps even the new 'essential power', post-corona. A power that was willing to cooperate with others to safeguard international public health. Xi Jinping's speech at the Extraordinary G20 Leaders' Summit in late March served exactly that purpose. It was a eulogy of the international community, the 'community of nations', that should 'strengthen confidence, act with unity and work together in a collective response'. 'Guided by the vision of building a community with a shared future for mankind', China was ready to share its good practices, conduct joint research on drugs and vaccines and provide assistance where it could to countries hit by the growing outbreak. According to the Chinese president, all international organisations that could play a role in that should be supported, starting with the WHO. He also called for more international macro-economic policy coordination. In that area too, China was willing to play its part. It would 'continue to advance reform and opening-up, widen market access, improve the business environment, and expand imports and outbound investment to contribute to a stable world economy'. The speech made me think of Xi's interventions at the World Economic Forum in Davos, in 2017 and 2019. There he positioned himself as the protector of globalisation and the champion of multilateralism. Under Chinese leadership, of course. China's position as the medical manufacturing shop of the world gave it the tools to underscore this leading position through a carefully planned programme of donating or selling medical supplies to countries that desperately needed them.

The US, on the other hand, went to great lengths to counter China's global ambitions. In multiple messages it portrayed China as a regime that had misled the US and the world. It could and should not be trusted. The US administration attacked China's overall lack of transparency. The fact that president Trump had praised China and its president at least fifteen times in January and February for its transparency and hard work had been quickly forgotten. Had China shared information sooner, 'it could have been stopped right where it came from, China', Trump said at a White House news conference in March. 'The world is paying a very big price for what they did'. The World Health Organization took its fair share of the blows. The 'very China-centric' WHO was an accomplice, according to the US, which decided to first suspend its funding to the organisation and then withdraw from it. In the midst of a global health crisis of unparalleled proportions.

A direct phone call between both presidents ('a very good conversation', according to Trump) only led to a temporary truce. In mid-April the American president confirmed that the US was doing a very thorough examination into 'multiple sources', saying that COVID-19 may have escaped from a Wuhan laboratory with weak safety protocols. Later that day, a new US government report was released, claiming that China may have secretly conducted underground nuclear test explosions. There was clearly a lack of transparency on the Chinese side, the report found. Different topic, same narrative. A narrative that easily found its way into Trump's presidential election campaign, which painted the rival candidate Joe Biden as being soft on China, and his son Hunter Biden as excessively involved in several business deals with the Chinese.

The US also reached out to the rest of the world. When several African diplomats in Beijing collectively condemned the fact that African nationals living in China were systematically treated as potential carriers of the coronavirus, and were severely harassed, they got immediate support from the US. In a message, the US embassy in Guangzhou warned that 'police ordered bars and restaurants not to serve clients who appear to be of African origin'. Local officials launched mandatory testing and self-quarantine for 'anyone with African contacts', the statement said. The US also had a message for Europe. In a call with European reporters, secretary of state Pompeo stated: 'There is no country in the world that will provide as much aid assistance as the US will'.

In conflicts such as this, truth is always the first victim. I will go deeper into that in chapter 14. Time will no doubt provide more answers as to which claims are closest to reality. At the request of the EU, the World Health Organization committed in mid-May to an impartial, independent and thorough investigation into the outbreak of the virus and the reaction of the WHO to it. China agreed to participate in such an investigation, once the crisis was over. In the meantime, scientists will continue their work, including looking into where the virus originated and how it was first transmitted to human beings. But while watching the epic battle of words between two powers with global ambitions unfold, two thoughts were constantly on my mind. The first one goes back to a plea of the WHO chief: 'Please do not politicise this virus,' he said. 'If you don't want many more body bags, then you refrain from politicising it.' Throughout the crisis, this would not only turn out to be a challenge in international politics but also in national politics. The second thought goes back to an old African proverb: 'If two elephants fight, it's the grass that suffers'. The grass is Europe, keen to occupy the middle ground between the two. In other words: where does Europe stand in all this?

Before we get there, there is one other question that has puzzled me right from the very beginning: 'Could we have seen this coming?'

CHAPTER 2

(Lack of) Foresight

- How the novel coronavirus relates to environmental policies
- How predictable this pandemic really was
- How fast viruses can spread and what R-naught means

A WORLD ON THE MOVE

Wuhan is a city of 11 million people, roughly the same as the population of Belgium. A city very well connected with major cities both inside and outside China. As one of China's most important railway hubs, it is served by high-speed trains that take you to Shanghai or Guangzhou in a matter of hours. Its main airport, Wuhan Tianhe International Airport, has direct flights to almost a hundred destinations in eighteen countries. With more than twenty million passengers a year, it is the busiest airport in Central China.

Viruses know no borders; they go where people go. The fact that the first infections outside China showed up in Thailand should not come as a surprise. With 11 million Chinese visitors a year (2019), it is a very popular holiday destination. Less than two weeks after China had informed the WHO about the outbreak of an 'unknown pneumonia', the first three cases were confirmed in Thailand, all of them Chinese tourists. Soon after, a 73-year-old Thai lady who had spent her Christmas holidays in Wuhan was confirmed as the first Thai patient. After a couple of days in the hospital, she was back on her feet.

Around the same time, Japan reported its first case: a man in his thirties who had visited Wuhan had tested positive. Hong Kong, South Korea, Taiwan, Singapore and Vietnam were not far behind. On the same day Japan confirmed its first case, 16 January, a 35-year-old American was on his way back from Wuhan to Washington State. He would be the first confirmed American patient. By then the virus' globe-trotting journey was well underway, as it accompanied tens of millions of people travelling to and from China to celebrate the Chinese New Year.

How fast a virus spreads is expressed in the term 'R0' (pronounced as 'R-naught'). A term that most of us – non-experts in virology that is – discovered around that time and one that would stay with us for most of the crisis. Put simply, R0 indicates how many people a single person who carries a virus will potentially infect. In the case of the COVID-19 virus, the R0 was somewhere between two and three. In other words: in a society that is not prepared and where no particular measures are taken, every infected person will spread the virus to – on average – two to three fellow humans.

The goal is to get this number under 1: when an infected person infects less than one other person, the virus inevitably slows down. An R0 between two and three is pretty much comparable to SARS and HIV (both between 2 and 5), more than the seasonal flu (around 1.3), but peanuts compared to measles, which has an R0 of between twelve and eighteen. As this last example shows, with the right measures, such as vaccinations, a high reproduction number does not have to mean a high number of infections in the real world. That's the good news: the virus could be slowed down, even without a vaccine.

When the new virus entered the picture, it found a global population without immunity (it was a new virus so no immunity could have been built up), without a vaccine, and without much knowledge about how the virus behaved. In little over two months, COVID-19 would spread to 29 countries. In the first two weeks of March, the number of cases outside China had increased 13-fold, and the number of countries affected had tripled. By 11 March, when the World Health Organization declared it a pandemic, there were 118,000 cases in 114 countries. More than 4000 people had died. It was the fifth pandemic since the Spanish flu in 1918, the first ever caused by a coronavirus.

FOCUS ON:

The pandemics

1918-19	Spanish flu	A(H1N1)	20-50 million †
1957-58	Asian flu	A(H2N2)	1-4 million †
1968	Hong Kong flu	A(H3N2)	1-4 million †
2009-10	swine flu ('Mexican flu')	A(H1N1)	150k-570k †
2019	COVID-19	SARS-CoV-2	?

Other outbreaks of the coronavirus include: 2002-2003 SARS (ca. 774 †) and 2012-2013 MERS (ca. 858 †). In comparison: seasonal flu kills ca. 500k annually. The HIV/AIDS virus has killed 32 million people since its outbreak in 1981.

Source: WHO, The Lancet.

A WORLD AT RISK

In the foresight reports that were my Christmas holiday reading, I occasionally saw references to the threat of pandemics. In the (excellent) report 'Global Trends to 2030: Challenges and Choices for Europe', published by an independent foresight group of members from the European institutions in April 2019, this passage caught my eye: 'As humans travel, so do the diseases they carry, increasing the risk of pandemics. While there has been progress on prevention and reporting, especially vulnerable states are lagging behind when it comes to important reforms in this regard.' But it continued: 'The majority of deaths, not just in Europe but also in the world, will be because of non-communicable diseases such as cancer or cardiovascular diseases.' This reference – the only one to diseases in the entire report – made total sense when I read it. Like most, if not all Europeans, I could easily name friends or family members who had died of cancer or a heart attack. The idea that in my lifetime Europeans would die in large numbers because of a pandemic, in all honesty had not crossed my mind.

Only after the pandemic hit us, did I notice how many studies and reports there were sounding the alarm bells. In a September 2019 report with the clue-is-in-the-title name 'A World at Risk', the WHO counted, during the previous seven years alone, almost 1500 epidemic events in 172 countries. These were the forerunners of 'a new era of high-impact, potentially fast-spreading outbreaks that are more frequently detected and increasingly difficult to manage'. Looking at the past, the report argued that 'there is a very real threat of a rapidly moving, highly lethal pandemic of a respiratory pathogen killing 50 to 80 million people and wiping out nearly 5% of the world's economy.' The World Economic Forum reached a similar conclusion: 'the number of epidemic events had increased over the past 30 years; the danger of a pandemic in the hyper-connected 21st century was higher than at most other times in human history'.

Even more specific were the annual threat analyses of the intelligence agencies of the United States, a country that spends more than $80 billion a year on intelligence gathering. In their 2017 and 2018 Worldwide Threat Analyses, they warned of the increasing risks of a global pandemic. They were remarkably explicit: 'A novel strain of a virulent microbe that is easily transmissible between humans continues to be a major threat, with pathogens such as (…) Middle East Respiratory Syndrome Coronavirus having pandemic potential if they were to acquire efficient human-to-human transmissibility'. The reason stated was also pretty accurate: 'the growing proximity of humans and animals (...) pathogens originally found in animals have spread to human populations'. Ten years earlier, three researchers raised a similar red flag in their study 'Severe Acute Respiratory Syndrome Coronavirus as an Agent of Emerging and Reemerging Infection': 'The presence of a large reservoir of Sars-CoV-like viruses in horseshoe bats, together with the culture of eating exotic mammals in southern China, is a timebomb'. The warning could not have been more explicit.

APOCALYPTIC PANDEMICS

In the expert community there was broad consensus that the outbreak of a global viral pandemic is much more likely now than in the past. Inevitable, even. Most experts also seemed to agree on why: we make it a lot easier for viruses to cross from animals to people. There are still many unknown viruses and diseases lurking in the planet's forests. As long as they stay there, there is no problem. But when wildlife is driven into contact with domestic animals and eventually humans, that's when the problems start.

That is exactly what is happening right now. Executive director of the United Nations Environment Programme Inger Andersen summed it up in March 2020: 'Never before have so many opportunities existed for pathogens to pass from wild and domestic animals to people'. Seventy-five percent of all emerging infectious diseases – Ebola, HIV, bird flu, MERS, SARS, the Rift Valley fever, the West Nile virus, the Zika virus – come from wildlife. COVID-19 was just the latest in a long line.

One important cause is deforestation. In 2018 alone, the tropics lost 12 million hectares, more than three times the size of Belgium. Forests partly vanish because we need more land to feed, house and satisfy the needs of our expanding global population. This is a megatrend that will particularly affect Africa and Asia, where expanding megacities change the way land is used. More people need more food, leading to more cattle breeding and agriculture, all of which eats into the forests. More people also means more devices, hence more raw materials. We build roads and cities, we grow palm oil and extract cobalt where there used to be forests. Another threat to forests are wildfires, which is where climate change comes in. It's fascinating, and worrisome, to see how everything is connected.

A good example is Indonesia, a fascinating country that I started to take an interest in some twenty years ago. Burning forests for agricultural production (palm oil) is a common practice there. The drought caused by runaway climate change makes these fires ever more dangerous. A well-documented case are the wildfires of 1997. That year, an area almost twice the size of Latvia went up in flames, destroying the habitat of large groups of animals. Including fruit bats. A year later, 105 people died in Malaysia, in what was the first outbreak of the Nipah virus in human beings. Until then, the virus had only been present in bats, the same bats that were forced out of the Indonesian forests. From Indonesia, some of them migrated to Malaysia. When pigs ate the fruit that bats had nibbled on, they got infected and transmitted the virus to a couple of local farmers. With this kind of chain of events going on, virologist reports are as much of a page-turner as a good detective story.

This broader context does not make it easier to prevent future pandemics. If the outbreak of COVID-19 was only the consequence of local culinary traditions or a lack of adequate sanitary provisions, then this could in theory be remedied. Albeit with Herculean effort. You could close down all wet markets where wildlife is sold, as the Chinese authorities did, at least temporarily, with the Huanan Seafood Wholefood Market on 1 January. Or you could introduce and consistently enforce legislation prohibiting the trade in and consumption of wildlife. But if the causes are more structural, then such measures alone will not be sufficient. Then a much broader discussion opens up, centred on several trade-offs between economic development and the way we handle our environment.

Let me briefly illustrate this, using one of my top ten favourite reads, Timothy Mitchell's 2002 book 'Rule of Experts. Egypt, Techno-Politics, Modernity'. Rule of Experts is a fascinating account of Egypt's efforts, since the mid-19th century, to build a network of canals, barrages and dams, of which the Aswan dam is by far the best known. The goal was to better control the unpredictable and often damaging natural flooding of the Nile and to store more water that could be used for irrigation. Farmland would be better protected, food security for Egypt's growing population would be improved and all that would contribute to more economic development.

Controlling the natural environment, in this case the Nile Valley, was important and even necessary, for the modernisation of Egypt. But what the engineers were not aware of, was that these changes to the natural environment would turn the region into a perfect breeding ground for mosquitoes carrying the malaria parasite Plasmodium falciparum. This, and some other factors, led to a major malaria outbreak which caused 100,000-200,000 deaths during the first three years of World War II. Such trade-offs between human engineering and the natural environment matter even more today than in the past. Knowing that by 2050 global demand for food, water and energy will rise dramatically, possibly by 50 to 60%, finding a balanced, sustainable approach to the way we handle our natural environment will be one of the main global challenges in the coming years. In my opinion, even the main one.

Other megatrends facilitate the outbreak of global pandemics. The world's rapidly increasing connectivity is an obvious one, illustrated by the fact that Chinese New Year caused around three billion car, train and plane trips within and to China. China is increasingly better connected with the rest of the world. Between 2005 and 2015, the number of international air routes from mainland China tripled from 233 to 739. In the same period, the annual number of air passengers travelling in and out of China increased 17-fold, from 3 to 51 million. Similar trends can be seen elsewhere. This hyperconnectivity, combined with denser urbanisation and the rise of megacities, means that the opportunities for the transmission of a viral disease have become almost endless.

This analysis is not new. The topic is regularly discussed by international policymakers. International fora such as the G7, the G20, the G77 or the African Union, to name but a few, regularly adopt political commitments on epidemic preparedness. In September 2018, the G77 foreign ministers acknowledged that epidemics or similar global health threats were due the same level of attention as other serious threats confronting their countries. Sometimes, the discussions became very concrete and practical. During their meeting in Berlin in May 2017, the health ministers of the G20 held a well-prepared simulation exercise. The scenario was pretty realistic, despite the somewhat creative name of the virus (the Mountain Associated Respiratory Syndrome, or MARS), and the place where the outbreak took place (in Anycountry and neighbouring Nexdoria). In the Berlin Declaration that was adopted after the session, the ministers recognised that because of the global interconnectedness of societies, businesses and governments, 'an infectious disease risk anywhere can become a health risk everywhere'. That summed it up pretty nicely.

So, what went wrong? Are virologists our version of the Cassandra who warned what was coming but nobody listened? The question is partly answered in the September 2019 volume of the journal *Foreign Policy*, just a couple of months before the outbreak. One article had the title: 'Apocalyptic Pandemic is Coming. But Nobody is interested in doing anything about it'. The article summarised the main conclusions of the World At Risk report. 'The world as a whole', it said, 'is not prepared. Preparedness is hampered by the lack of continued political will at all levels. Although national leaders respond to health crises when fear and panic grow strong enough, most countries do not devote the consistent energy and resources needed to keep outbreaks from escalating into disasters.'

That was also the message of Yale historian Frank Snowden who in October 2019, just months before the recent COVID-19 outbreak, published a very persuasive book Epidemics and Society. From the Black Death to the Present (great timing but he can already add an extra chapter). In his book he quoted a report written by the US Department of Defense from 1998, more than twenty years ago: 'Historians in the next millennium may find that the twentieth century's greatest fallacy was the belief that infectious diseases were nearing elimination. The resultant complacency has actually increased the threat'. And in January 2020 at Davos, when the new coronavirus was slowly but discretely conquering the world, one of the speakers shared exactly the same conclusion with the powerful audience. 'We know what we need to do', the head of the Coalition for Epidemic Preparedness Innovations Richard Hatchett said. 'The question is whether we have the political will to do it and whether we choose to allocate the resources that are required.'

Resources remain a precondition for solid public health programmes dealing with communicable diseases. This is especially so now that focus has shifted to other deadly diseases. Globally, more people die from eating too much than from not eating enough. This is one of the reasons why there are more cases of diabetes, heart diseases and cancer. This also requires resources. But, Hatchett continued, it is not only about resources. 'Governments have to recognise that individual governments working by themselves will not be able to solve this problem. They have to pool their resources and pool their efforts.' That's another important element: pooling resources, pooling efforts, in short: cooperation. That brings us quite nicely to the next chapter, in which we see what happens when the new virus hits the European Union. The European Union, which up until now has been the most concrete and successful example of governments pooling their resources and efforts.

CHAPTER 3

The Power to Act

- How COVID-19 invaded the European Union
- How the European Union can fight a pandemic
- How prepared the European Union really was

A FIRST MINI-WAVE, THE PRELUDE

From Wuhan there were three direct flights a week to Rome, three to London and six to Paris. These three countries were therefore alert and watchful, but all in all self-confident. The virus was first and foremost an epidemic in China, at most Asia. At a press conference on 21 January, the then French health minister Agnès Buzyn summarised the general mood as follows: 'The risk that the virus will be introduced in France is small but cannot be excluded, especially since there are direct flights from Wuhan'. And she added in the same breath: 'Our health system is well-prepared and the health institutions are informed'. People on direct flights to and from Wuhan were provided with information, including on what to do in case they had any symptoms.

But barely 72 hours later, she had to give another press conference, this time to announce the first confirmed case in Bordeaux, France (and with it, Europe): a 48-year-old Frenchman of Chinese origin. Three months later, French researchers who had taken a fresh look at old medical cases found out that the virus had already been around for some time. New tests showed that a patient who was treated in a Parisian hospital on 27 December had been infected with the coronavirus, but that would only be revealed in early May. Until then, 24 January would go down in the history books as the day Europe's first confirmed case became a fact.

The same day, some 600 kilometres further north in France, two other patients were taken to a Parisian hospital. All three patients had just travelled to China. The French government immediately took action. To contain the spread, they started tracing people with whom the patients had been in contact. All people who had recently been to China and had symptoms were advised to contact a medical emergency service. The mayor of Bordeaux decided to cancel the Chinese New Year festivities that were scheduled to take place the following weekend in his city. Closing the borders for passengers coming from China was not an option (yet), but incoming flights from China got special treatment at the airport, and passengers on these flights were isolated as much as possible from each other. Meanwhile, the French foreign minister was already thinking about French citizens stuck in Wuhan, and how to repatriate them.

France did not remain the only affected European country for long. On Monday 27 January, Germany reported its first cases. Finland followed two days later, as did the UK, where two Chinese nationals fell ill in the city of York. By the end of the week, the first two cases had been detected in Italy (Rome): two Chinese tourists who had arrived in Milan a week earlier and had travelled to Rome on a tourist bus. On 31 January, Spain got its first case, on the Canary Island of La Gomera, and Sweden joined in too: a young woman who had visited Wuhan. Belgium wrapped up this first mini-wave with its first confirmed patient on 3 February: a Belgian returning from Wuhan. After this first flurry, it wouldn't be until the 25 February before other EU countries were confronted with the virus. What was reassuring: most of the cases in this first wave were either directly linked to China or to two main clusters, one in Bavaria, another one in Haute-Savoie. This at least made the situation pretty straightforward to follow.

In those last days of January, politicians and experts alike repeatedly stressed that 'the EU was ready, the EU was prepared'. But how prepared could the EU be, given the limited competences the Union had in the field of health? Before looking at how the EU actually handled the COVID-19 crisis, let's see which tools the EU had (and has) at its disposal.

HEALTH POLICY: WHO CALLS THE SHOTS IN EUROPE?

At first glance, the EU has no medical superpowers. In the area of health policy, national governments have traditionally been very cautious not to shift too much power to the European level. The way health care is organised and financed is often the result of a very specific national tradition or particular ideological choices. When you are sick in Belgium, you choose your own doctor, you make an appointment and after the visit you pay around 25% of the medical costs. The rest is taken care of by an organisation called a 'mutuality'. I'll stop there before I lose you with the ins and outs of this somewhat complex system that has its roots in Belgian history. But the same goes for all EU countries. In practice, this diversity leads to very different realities throughout Europe. Some countries reimburse homeopathic treatment, others don't. In some countries, homeopathic therapy is regulated, in others not.

These and other choices are so much linked to the social security systems of the country – an area in which huge sums of money are passed around – that they prefer to keep decision-making in their own hands. When the new European Treaty – the Bible of what the European Union can and cannot decide – was negotiated, the countries made this crystal clear: 'Union action', article 168 stated, 'shall respect the responsibilities of the Member States for the definition of their health policy and for the organization and delivery of health services and medical care. The responsibilities of the Member States shall include the management of health services and medical care and the allocation of the resources assigned to them.' It couldn't be clearer really: how medical care is organised, and paid for, is up the countries themselves (referred to officially as Member States).

FOCUS ON:

The Lisbon Treaty

In a European treaty, the countries that form the European Union agree on which decisions have to be taken at the national level, and which decisions have to be taken at the European level. Such a treaty describes in detail how the Union functions. When several new countries joined the EU, it was time to update the 1958 Rome Treaty and the 1992 Maastricht Treaty. That's what the Lisbon Treaty did. It was signed in December 2007 and entered into force on 1 January 2009. It stated that in some policy areas the EU was 'exclusively' responsible while in others the EU and the countries had a shared responsibility. Then there was a third group of policy areas where the countries take the main decisions, with the support of the EU. Health policy belongs to that third category.

Unlike other areas such as trade or agricultural policy, where the European Union has more power, in the area of health policy, the most the EU can do is 'complement' national policies. This means that the EU can help governments to coordinate their policies or come up with guidelines. It can also make sure that what works well in one country is shared with other countries. This limited remit is also reflected by its limited budget: 450 million euros for the period 2014-2020, out of a total budget of 960 billion. Less than 65 million a year.

At the same time, the EU countries know all too well that not everything can be handled at the national level. It can even be in their interests to involve the European level. Usually this awareness increases in the midst of a health crisis. This was the case after the 1991 blood scandal in France, where blood products contaminated with HIV were distributed to more than 4000 people. Or after multiple incidents involving defective hip replacements, not unimportant for Europe's ageing population.

The EU, the countries agreed, should therefore set European-wide, legally binding, enforceable standards for the quality and safety of – to stick to these examples – blood products and medical devices. A health crisis also tends to lead to the creation of new European institutions. When the mad cow disease and its human variant Creutzfeldt-Jakob broke out in 1994, it eventually led to the creation of the European Food Safety Authority, in 2002. Its mandate was precisely to come up with independent scientific advice to protect the safety of the food chain and to prevent future outbreaks of Creutzfeldt-Jakob, salmonella contaminations or other food risks.

Part of the EU's role in health policy is indirect. It is derived from the EU's power to legislate in other areas that have an indirect impact on national health policy. To guarantee the free movement of people, workers who move to another EU country for their job have access to health care services in that other country. To guarantee the free movement of goods, pharmaceutical products need to respect the same standards in the entire European single market. European legislation to improve air quality, to set safety procedures on the work floor or to impose food labelling – areas where the EU plays a major role – also has a huge impact on our health. If Europe funds research to lower the risk of transplant rejection, it will have an impact on many ageing Europeans. And if we can now go to a bar or a restaurant without being suffocated by cigarette smoke (apologies to the smokers), then it is because Europe took action to fight cancer and lung diseases. Through all of these policies – environmental, research, consumer protection, single market – the impact of the European Union on our health is substantial.

When it comes to managing epidemics or handling medical emergencies, however, the EU has no direct legislative powers. It cannot tell countries what to do. It cannot decide how they should organise their hospitals, how many intensive care beds they should foresee or how they should prepare their test labs. The EU can only give advice.

In the past, this has not prevented the EU from continuously expanding its role in this area. Each virus outbreak has led to new initiatives. The SARS outbreak in 2002-2003 is a good example. Europe was largely spared by this epidemic. Of the almost 800 people who died of the virus, only one person died in Europe, in France. But the threat was real enough for the EU to create a new agency in 2004, the European Centre for Disease Control (with its rock-solid abbreviation ECDC). The name might suggest otherwise, but this was not the European version of the all-powerful CDC, the Center for Disease Control and Prevention in the US. If you see doctors in an American film racing to find a vaccine or to control a pandemic that risks wiping out the entire human race, they will likely be in CDC uniforms. In times of crisis it has huge authority, at least under previous American presidents.

In the EU it's different. In line with the clear division of power in the EU, the main responsibility for preventing, monitoring and handling a viral outbreak is at the national level, with the EU countries. The ECDC would be able to monitor and coordinate the national efforts, collect information, do research and collect scientific data on how best to react to an outbreak. At most it could help countries build up capacity through training programmes and by sharing technical expertise. But what it couldn't do is impose the measures it thought were needed to control an epidemic. Compared to its American counterpart, it is small, both in resources and staff. With an annual budget of 58 million euros and 290 employees, it is in a different league to the CDC, with its $7 billion dollar budget and 12000 employees.

The swine flu or Mexican flu that travelled around the globe throughout most of 2009, was a different kind of threat. This H1N1 virus, which was closely related to the virus that caused the deadly Spanish flu in 1918-1920, did make it to Europe. Officially, it killed some 2900 Europeans, although real figures were probably much higher.

In that period, I was working at the Permanent Representation of Belgium to the European Union. The entire team was fully involved in the preparation of the Belgian presidency of the Council, which started on 1 July 2010. The Belgian presidency hit the ground running by organising a 'pandemic lessons learned' conference in its first two days in action. Some of the recommendations that came out of that conference could have been written now. One of the recommendations was to harmonise the way EU countries report on the number of infections and deaths during a pandemic.

Ten years later, the methodological differences are still considerable. There is EU legislation that obliges countries to report cases of infectious diseases to the ECDC. But which cases (only confirmed cases based on testing or also suspected cases?) or how these cases should be reported remains the responsibility of the countries. The ECDC can only give guidance. That is what the ECDC did in the corona crisis. Countries that followed these guidelines typically ended up with higher COVID-19 mortality figures than those that did not. This not only creates confusion; it also hampers coordinated monitoring and action.

'WE ARE PREPARED'

Other recommendations made in 2010, however, were implemented. The lessons learned exercise after the swine flu crisis led for instance to the creation of new tools that now played an important role in the fight against COVID-19, and that improved the EU's preparedness. One of them was a mechanism to jointly purchase vaccines and medication. Another one was the strengthening of the Health Security Committee. This committee was created in 2001, in response to the 9/11 terrorist attacks. It was created as an informal forum where senior representatives of the EU countries' health departments, together with the European Commission, could coordinate their response to health-related threats linked to terrorist or biological attacks. Later, its mandate was extended to include pandemics.

In the years after the 2009 pandemic, the EU focused more than ever on increasing its preparedness for a new pandemic. In 2014, it started funding a clinical research network that covered some 600 primary care sites and 600 hospitals in 27 EU countries: the 'Platform for European Preparedness Against (Re-)emerging Epidemics' (with a handy acronym: PREPARE). The idea behind this initiative was to ensure that in case of a new outbreak, clinical research across Europe could start immediately, without any unnecessary delays: 'We need to know how it spreads, who is most at risk, how severe the disease is, and how patients are best diagnosed and treated,' explained Professor Peter Horby of the University of Oxford and a member of PREPARE. When you fight an enemy, the sooner you know how it behaves and the sooner you uncover its weaknesses, the faster you will win.

So, much work was done, mainly after the H1N1 outbreak. This explains why, when the first cases were detected in Europe, most experts were relatively sure that the EU was well prepared. The very first Global Health Security Index, published in October 2019 by the Johns Hopkins Center for Health Security, the Economist Intelligence Unit and the Nuclear Threat Initiative, revealed that amongst the 195 countries analysed, European countries were doing rather well in terms of pandemic preparedness. Twelve countries in the top 20 were

EU countries. Its overall, much less-reassuring message – 'collectively, international preparedness is weak' – got about the same amount of media attention as the other reports we saw in chapter 2: too little.

The feeling of being prepared was broadly shared within the European Union. At a scientific meeting in Brussels, organised by PREPARE in September 2018, professor of infectious diseases at Paris Diderot University, Yazdan Yazdanpanah, said that in the event of a serious pandemic 'we would be prepared more than before, but we can always do better'. This was echoed by others. 'Overall', Daniela Braun of the Konrad Adenauer Foundation argued in July 2019, 'Europe is currently better prepared for a severe epidemic or pandemic than it was just a few years ago'.

The ECDC made a similar assessment in the first days of the outbreak: 'Most EU countries have plans and measures in place to contain this kind of infection and Europe has well-equipped laboratories that can confirm probable cases in addition to hospitals that are prepared to treat patients accordingly.' And it added: 'In the past, systematic implementation and infection prevention and control measures were effective in controlling both SARS-CoV and MERS-CoV. (...) Even if there are still many things unknown about 2019-nCoV, European countries have the necessary capacities to prevent and control an outbreak as soon as cases are detected.'

Some of these observers did spot some weaknesses. Daniela Braun identified the lack of coordination as a major challenge: 'EU weaknesses in the area of reaction to pandemics are especially great when it comes to coordinating individual EU measures and among member states'. She also warned that years of austerity measures, a result of the 2007-2008 economic and financial crisis, had an impact on health systems, especially in Eastern and Central Europe. This had possibly widened the already sharp differences between Member States, not only in terms of capacity, but also in terms of regulations.

In hindsight, I see two other take-aways from the previous major health crises and the EU's preparedness. The first: for politicians, doing too much could be as harmful as not doing enough. When the 2009 swine flu pandemic turned out to be less dramatic than most experts had warned, several governments and the EU as a whole were heavily criticised for having over-reacted. Too much money was wasted, too much panic had been created, and all for no good reason, the criticism went. In its 2010 assessment, the Parliamentary Assembly of the Council of Europe stated quite bluntly: 'The handling of the pandemic by the World Health Organization, EU Health Agencies and national governments led to a waste of large sums of public money, and unjustified scares and fears about the health risks faced by the European public'. France had ordered close to 100 million vaccines, but in the end only six million Frenchmen were vaccinated. Some opponents went as far as to suggest that the purchase of vaccines was driven by the pharmaceutical industry, eager to sell as many vaccines as possible. When a new virus breaks out, politicians and experts who know their history also know that their decisions and advice should be proportionate.

My second take-away is that as soon as the swine flu pandemic broke out, there was a rush by individual EU countries on vaccines. Some bought what they could, showing very few intentions to share with others. In its 2014 study 'Everything you always wanted to know about European Union health policies but were afraid to ask', the European Observatory on Health Systems and Policies came to a blunt conclusion: 'Historically, crisis response and management has been the weak point of European action on health threats. Faced with urgent situations and domestic pressures, Member State governments have tended to revert to taking national measures, sometimes even against the interest of other Member States.' In other words, in times of stress, solidarity is fragile. Just how fragile would soon become clear.

CHAPTER 4

On the Ministers' Agenda

- Why France wanted a European reaction
- Why airport policies differed so much across the EU
- Why ministers took their time to react

FIRST, THE AMBASSADORS

Whether COVID-19 would also reach European soil depended on how contagious it was. Even before China had officially confirmed human to human transmission on 20 January, the European Centre for Disease Control considered it very likely that the virus could jump from one person to another. There was no clear indication yet that this was the case, but 'it may have occurred', the agency wrote rather diplomatically on 17 January. If that were the case, the virus could spread fast. So the first challenge was to make it as difficult as possible for the virus to enter Europe. Easier said than done. In an average month, some 300,000 people travel to Europe from mainland China. Even more so in January, with Chinese New Year. Therefore the second challenge was at least as important: once the virus was in Europe, it had to be slowed down. The goal now was to save time. Time that virologists from all over the world could use to uncover the newcomer's secrets. In early January, the Chinese had shared the genetic data with the global community of virologists so they could all start looking for clues on how to detect it, and eventually how to cure it. That was the battle plan.

For French decision-makers this battle plan from the beginning needed a European component. That was exactly the message that the then French health minister Agnès Buzyn gave the 21 January. 'The answer must be European because you can have a person who arrives in Brussels and then travels to France by road'. To slow down a viral outbreak, all EU countries would have to be on board, she said, just three days before the first COVID cases were confirmed.

It was France that first brought COVID-19 to the European political agenda. When an EU country wants to bring a topic to the attention of the other EU countries, it has several options. One of the easiest ways is to raise it in the Committee of Permanent Representatives, the so-called COREPER (derived from the French Comité des Représentants Permanents). This Committee is the engine room in which the ambassadors of all EU countries forge their individual national positions into one single Council position. They meet at least once a week, usually several days a week, in Brussels' Justus Lipsius building just across the road from the Berlaymont where the European Commission is based. All possible topics that affect Europe (are there many that don't?) pass by at some point, from agricultural policy to climate change, from migration to education, from transport to economic sanctions.

On 27 January, after all the other agenda items had been discussed, the French ambassador asked for the floor. He wanted to add one more item before they all left the room: corona. This was the first time the virus infiltrated the European agenda. The situation in Wuhan is worrisome, the ambassador said. Fifty-six people had died, the virus was spreading fast in the Wuhan region and drastic emergency measures had been put in place. Wuhan International Airport had been closed; all public transport in the area was suspended; places where many people meet, like markets, internet cafés, cinemas, entertainment parks or cultural sites were closed. These were draconian measures that affected more than twenty million people in more than ten cities in the Wuhan area. This was not only very difficult for the Chinese inhabitants, it was also problematic for European citizens who lived there or were there on business. Since all commercial flights were cancelled, these people were stuck in the city. France was planning one or more repatriation flights to bring French citizens home. Capacity allowing, the flight would also be open to citizens from other EU countries, the ambassador offered. 'Let's coordinate', was his message.

In response to the French initiative, the presidency of COREPER, which was for the first six months of 2020 in the hands of the Croatian ambassador, scheduled a follow-up meeting for that very afternoon. The main goal was to discuss how this coordinated effort could be best organised. There was widespread consensus that to respond to the French request, information had to flow faster between EU countries and between them and the European institutions. Decisions and communications had to be well prepared to make sure that both were coherent; the chain of command had to be streamlined.

When the ambassadors met that afternoon, they quickly agreed that the best way to exchange information was through the 'Integrated Political Crisis Response' (IPCR, for short). This was a relatively new tool, or rather a relatively new way of working. For most of the history of the European Union, crisis response had been a national competence. The European Union played a secondary role, a supporting role. But in the wake of the 9/11 terrorist attacks, the 2004 Madrid train bombings and the 2005 London bombings, this somewhat changed. The idea that the European Union should play a bigger role in emergency situations gained ground. There was a logic to it: if in a crisis every EU country takes its own measures or waits to see what others are doing, valuable time is lost. By 2013 (there was clearly no sense of urgency) this awareness led to the creation of the IPCR. The first – and until now only – time the IPCR was used was during the 2015 refugee and migration crisis.

The IPCR was by no means a magic wand. By formally activating the IPCR for the corona crisis, the EU countries first and foremost wanted to show that the issue was on their political radar, but they also wanted to get more control over developments. In a first phase, the IPCR would be used to bring all relevant actors together – the countries, the Commission, the European External Action Service (EEAS) and the cabinet of the President of the European Council. This would make it easier for them to share and compare the information they had, for instance on the number of Europeans that were stranded in Wuhan. All this information would be compiled and analysed by the Commission and the EEAS in regular analytical notes. Nothing more, but also nothing less.

GOVERNMENTS IN CHARGE

On the ground, each country took its own measures to keep the virus out. With a kind of domino effect, they changed their travel advice. On 28 January, the day the IPCR was activated, the British Foreign Office urged British citizens to avoid all but essential travel to mainland China. British Airways cancelled all its flights to China, including to Beijing and Shanghai. Soon after, following similar travel advice by the German government, the German airline Lufthansa and the affiliated Swiss and Austrian Airlines followed British Airways' example, cutting their flights to and from mainland China. The next day, another big European airline, Air France, scrapped all its flights to and from Wuhan but its flights to Shanghai and Beijing remained operational. France only issued negative travel advice for China a week after Germany had done so. There was one country that was first to go much further than all the others: Italy. On 30 January, Italy completely closed all its air traffic to and from China. As part of its state of emergency, all flights – without exception – between Italy and China were suspended, with immediate effect, after two Chinese tourists tested positive in Rome.

In the airports too, national policies differed. At Heathrow Airport, separate sections were created for passengers flying in from Chinese risk areas, so that they could be isolated from the rest of Heathrow. Italy organised thermo-screenings at several of its airports. Around that time, I was on a trip to Italy. When I arrived at Amerigo Vespucci airport in Florence, I was welcomed by a health officer who pointed a thermometer gun at my forehead. When I landed back into Brussels Airport, there was no screening at all. Not all of these national decisions were in line with the advice given by the World Health Organization or the European experts in the European Centre for Disease Control. On the same day that Italy banned all flights to China, the WHO declared the coronavirus an international emergency, but it also said explicitly that there was no reason to restrict or cancel flights. On the contrary, this could even be counterproductive since it would disrupt aid supplies. A day later, the ECDC gave similar advice to EU countries. Of course, travellers to China had to be informed of the risks of infection. They should avoid direct contact with live animals when visiting live markets in areas currently experiencing cases of the novel coronavirus. They should not consume raw or undercooked animal products, avoid contact with sick persons and regularly wash their hands. But restricting international traffic? Not necessary according to the ECDC. On thermo-screenings at airports, it was equally clear: these were not useful, definitely not in the midst of the seasonal flu season. The symptoms of COVID-19 and the normal flu were too similar for a simple temperature check to have real added value. It was not the first time, and would not be the last time, that experts and political decision-makers came to different conclusions.

The lack of European coordinated action, despite the activation of the Integrated Political Crisis Response, did not go unnoticed. It was definitely not appreciated by the European Parliament. On 3 February, at a meeting of the parliamentary committee in charge of health issues, Peter Liese, a German member of parliament and a medical doctor himself, regretted that some countries were making up their own rules: 'Italy has decided to cancel all flights from and to China and at the same time in the neighbouring countries, this is not the case. The virus doesn't respect national borders: either it is necessary, and every Member State should do it, or it is exaggerated, and then we should encourage Italy to be more flexible.

His colleague Milan Brglez, a newly elected member of parliament from Slovenia, was even more blunt: 'There is a lack of coordination', he stated. One way to improve coordination, according to several committee members, was to strengthen the ECDC. Based on the discussion in the parliamentary committee, the committee chair sent a letter to the Commission and the Croatian presidency of the Council, in which he reiterated that it was the European Parliament's call to give the ECDC a more powerful role. That was for sure music to the ears of its executive director Andrea Ammon, who had attended the committee meeting. She was rather positive about the situation itself: 'Right now', she said, 'it doesn't look like someone needs to be worried. We still consider that for Europe the risk is low. (…) Coordination within the EU but also with third countries has improved compared to previous crises'. Here she referred to the daily contact between her agency and the Commission, but also its counterparts in, for instance, China and the US.

FOCUS ON:

The European Parliament

The European Parliament has 705 members of parliament. When the European Commission makes a proposal for European legislation, it is the European Parliament that negotiates this with the Council of Ministers until there is an agreement. To prepare its plenary discussions, the Parliament has 20 committees, each in charge of certain topics. One of the most important committees in recent years is the ENVI Committee, in charge of environment policy, health and food safety. It has 69 members.

UP TO THE MINISTERS

In hindsight, Ammon's assessment might be considered surprising. But at that moment, there were only 23 confirmed cases in the EU. Worldwide, 362 people had died and all except one in China. For the time being, the situation seemed very much under control. The ambassadors had discussed it in COREPER, but it had not gone yet to the level just above it: the ministers. Some had asked that the ministers would get personally involved in handling the COVID-19 crisis. In the last days of January, European health commissioner Stella Kyriakides, who has a medical background, had been calling for this. In her own country, Cyprus, she had worked as a clinical psychologist for the Ministry of Health. Before joining the European Commission, she had also played a leading role in the fight against cancer. In her press conference on 30 January, she repeated her call for an extraordinary meeting of the Health Council, in which all EU countries were represented at ministerial level. But there was no immediate follow-up.

Besides the clear lack of a sense of urgency, there was another reason why the commissioner and the Italian, German and French health ministers, who also asked for a meeting, still had to exercise patience. The decision of whether to set up a meeting of the Council is the responsibility of the country that holds the presidency of the Council. It was therefore on the Croatian health minister to call the meeting. But as luck wouldn't have it, he had been fired in late January for his involvement in a real estate scandal. According to prime minister Andrej Plenkovic, 'the minister was focused on topics that had nothing to do with what he was doing.' Only when his successor was in place, could the Council be convened.

The ministers finally spoke to each other in the second

week of February. Their two meetings, first an informal video conference on 7 February, then a formal Council meeting a week later, give a good idea of the general mood in Europe at that moment. When the ministers met on 13 February, there were 44 confirmed cases in Europe. Not a single European had died from COVID-19. Most if not all countries confirmed that they were prepared. Hardly anyone reported a lack of medical equipment, such as face masks or protective gloves. Some, like France, Hungary and Spain even sent protective equipment to China, as a sign of solidarity. It was only later on that it became clear that many countries did not in fact have a precise idea of how many supplies they actually had.

Some smaller countries, like the Benelux countries, were more cautious. They did not rule out that, in the event of a real crisis, they might run out. That's why they asked to launch a group purchase of protective equipment, just to be on the safe side. Another problem that was raised, but more for the future, was that in case of a long-term 'closure' of China, the supply of medicines or ingredients to produce medicines might be disrupted. But no one considered this an immediate concern. The ECDC summarised this positive atmosphere as: 'containment is working.' Everything seemed under control. The main concern of many ministers around the table was to avoid panic. In that period between late January and early February, politicians and experts alike bombarded the public with the same message: Don't panic. After all, the seasonal flu kills far more people than the new coronavirus. The first meetings of the ministers were therefore rather consensual. The only issue they clashed on during their 13 February meeting was how to better coordinate the safety measures at the national airports. The Italian health minister tried to convince his colleagues to take tough measures, like thermo-screenings, in all major European airports, as was the case in some Italian airports. But he was talking to a brick wall. No country wanted to turn this policy into a European measure. Other ministers around the table suggested that passengers who arrived in a European airport should be put in quarantine.

But this also met with opposition. Each country should decide this for itself, several ministers argued. The German minister surprised his colleagues with yet another proposal. All travellers who arrived at a European airport should declare whether they had been in contact with people who could be suspected of carrying the virus. The fact that not only suspected or infected people but every traveller had to report on their whereabouts was a bridge too far for many ministers. In the end, they settled on a compromise: travellers arriving or in transit from affected areas could be asked to confirm whether they have been in contact with persons from risky areas where justified by circumstances (a phrase often used by diplomats to create maximum flexibility). But only Germany introduced this form of contact tracing. The fact that emergency health response was still a national and not a European responsibility could hardly have been better illustrated.

CHAPTER 5

'In Quarantena'

- Why the virus hit Italy so hard
- How populist parties tried to use COVID-19 for their own agenda
- How COVID-19 was able to spread all over Europe

BACK TO BUSINESS

After the meeting of the health ministers on 13 February, the European political agenda went back to normal. On COVID-19, the main concerns at that moment were not so much health-related. Apart from the fate of European citizens in China, European decision-makers worried most about the possible economic impact of the Chinese lockdown. China's official economic figures for the first two months of 2020 were dramatic. Compared to January and February 2019, investments had fallen by 25%. In several provinces, closed shops meant sales were down more than 20%. The temporary closure of factories led to a drop in industrial production of more than 13%. Exports were down 16% and unemployment reached its highest level in decades: 6.2%. Some slowdown in economic growth was to be expected also before the virus hit, as China's population gets older and its wages go up.

The trade conflict with the United States also made itself felt. In 2019, Chinese GDP growth was the slowest since 1990. But an economic standstill like this one, with more than 500 million people directly affected by lockdown measures, was in a league of its own.

The impact on Europe's economy could be considerable, as China is the undisputed engine of global economic growth. In the past couple of years, more than one third of the entire world's GDP growth was made in China. Double what the US and more than four times what the EU contributed to global growth. COVID-19 made that Chinese engine sputter. On top of that, no flights means no Chinese tourists. As they usually make over 115 million overseas trips a year, this was bad news for Europe's hotels and restaurants. And when China, the second largest importer in the world and the EU's second biggest trading partner, consumes less, European companies sell less. Car producers sell fewer cars, European fashion designers sell less luxury clothing. All reasons for European economists to keep a close eye on China's $14 trillion economy.

But apart from this, the issues that had dominated the agenda at the beginning of the year continued to keep ambassadors, European commissioners and parliamentarians busy. All in all, their regular work had hardly been affected, let alone derailed, by the COVID-19 outbreak. The Brexit fall-out was still absorbing a lot of energy. On the final day of January 2020, the UK formally left the EU. Negotiations on the new relationship between the European Union and the United Kingdom had started. They promised to be very difficult and – again – time consuming. In the Syrian province of Idlib, a humanitarian disaster was unfolding, one of the worst of the Syrian crisis. The Syrian regime, supported by Russian aircraft, continued its attempts to reconquer the entire country, forcing another one million Syrians to leave their homes. Turkish President

Erdoğan announced that he would no longer stop Syrian refugees at the Turkish borders, which opened a gateway to Europe. A new migration crisis was looming. Closer to home, a decision on EU membership negotiations with North Macedonia and Albania was long overdue. Within the EU itself, countries were discussing how to fund their ambition to make Europe carbon neutral by 2050. But the one issue that really kept decision- and opinion-makers busy in February was the so-called Multiannual Financial Framework (MFF), or in simpler terms: the 7-year budget of the European Union. MFF negotiations are by far the most complicated ones at the European level. It is here that decisions are made about how much money will go towards areas such as research, agriculture and the Erasmus+ programme over the coming years. It also decides how much EU countries will have to pay into the common budget, and how much they can take out. Fortunately, this exercise does not occur every year!

When the last 7-year budget was negotiated, the one for the period 2014-2020, I was working at the cabinet of then European Council president Herman Van Rompuy, who led the negotiations. The final phase of such negotiations is usually filled with drama, with all European leaders locked in the same room for marathon sessions. Sessions that are only interrupted by intensive bilateral side discussions in which many a prime minister or president tries to explain, passionately or calmly, why they cannot go back home with the proposal on the table. Like-minded countries form small groups, trying to steer the discussion in the direction they favour. Experts run in and out with new calculations and Excel files. They know all too well that if they give some extra euros to one country, they have to take it away from another. In the end, back then, it took two dramatic sessions of the

European Council, one in November 2012 and another in February 2013, to reach a compromise. When the last millions fell into place, you could feel the relief in the room. On 8 February, and after 24 hours of uninterrupted discussions, President Van Rompuy and his head of cabinet Didier Seeuws were able to go to the press room and present the deal to journalists.

Seven years later, in February 2020, negotiations on the new budget for 2021-2027 were also in their final phase. But this time, they were even more complex. The European Commission had presented its proposal back in May 2018. Since then, much groundwork had been done, on all possible levels. Hundreds of experts had looked into it, calculating what the Commission's figures actually meant for their country. As a result, the differences between the 27 EU countries had become much clearer, but not necessarily easier to bridge. The traditional money for agriculture and less developed regions remained very important for some countries. But at the same time, new priorities had emerged, and these also needed fresh funding. Climate change, for instance, or Europe's digital agenda. And could Europe really afford not to spend considerably more on migration, after the dramatic migration crisis of 2015? In short, more money was needed, but less money was available. The exit of the British, the biggest net contributor of the EU, also meant a loss of some 70 billion euros for the Union.

To square this circle, the 27 European leaders agreed to meet in Brussels on 20 and 21 February. One of the main sticking points was whether the new budget should be 1.070% of the European GDP, or 1.074%? Or only 1%, as some leaders argued? To an outsider it might look like splitting hairs, but strategic choices had to be made. Not all leaders around the table were prepared to do that (yet). After two days of negotiations, the leaders still weren't on the same page. On the Friday evening, European Council president Charles Michel wrapped up the meeting. 'We need more time', he concluded.

ALL EYES ON ITALY

When the Italian prime minister Giuseppe Conte left the European Council meeting that evening, journalists were not only interested in the budget discussions. They were at least as interested in the situation in Italy. That day the number of people infected with the COVID virus had gone up from three to seventeen, mostly in the Lombardy region, in the towns of Codogno and Castiglione d'Adda, and in the Veneto region. This number was higher than in any other European country. But perhaps even more worrisome: most of those infected had never set foot in China, unlike the first three confirmed cases in Italy. Prime minister Conte tried to reassure the journalists, and maybe also himself: 'We are prepared for this. We have a plan and we are implementing it', he replied. 'We have it under control'.

In reality, Italy stood then on the brink of a horrible weekend. By Monday, the number of infected Italians had topped 200. Six people had died. The numbers grew exponentially. The Italian government reacted with tough measures. A dozen municipalities in Lombardy and Veneto, two regions that represent one third of Italy's GDP, went into an immediate lockdown. Checkpoints manned by the police and army controlled all roads in. Churches suspended mass. Carnivals were cancelled. Sport activities were postponed. Bars, cinemas, theatres and most shops had to close. Universities paused all their activities. Streets were deserted. Anyone breaking the rules faced hefty fines or even prison.

Despite these measures, the figures continued to go up. A

week later, the death toll had increased five-fold, to thirty. At the end of March the death toll in Italy would pass 10,000. By then, the entire country, 60 million people, had been put in lockdown. 'Un intero paese in quarantena' (an entire country in quarantine), *La Repubblica* wrote. 'When the contagion arrived, in full force, it left us all stunned', the Italian author Paolo Giordano explained in his account 'How Contagion Works', which was flying off the (virtual) shelves.

The pace and brutality of the outbreak in Italy came as a surprise. Probably the most honest reaction came from Hans Kluge, the European director of the WHO. In an interview in *La Repubblica*, he said: 'In Italia i contagi sono un mistero'. It was a mystery 'that could have happened anywhere', ECDC director Andrea Ammon said, echoing his thoughts. The reason why it was Italy that was hit led to much speculation. Some scientists suspected that so-called super-spreaders might have been at work, people who infect up to thirty people instead of the usual two or three. Others, like the World Health Organization and prime minister Conte explained that in Italy health policy was organised on a regional level, not a national one. This made it more difficult to enforce all the rules everywhere with the same rigour. It was clear that the governor of Lombardy Attilio Fontana, a member of the right-wing Lega party, was not on the same wavelength as the national government. On 25 February he told the regional parliament that COVID-19 was 'just a little more than the normal flu'. He wanted to relax the lockdown. The mayor of Milan, from the leftist PD party, even launched the campaign 'Milan doesn't stop'. Another explanation that was often heard was that the local hospital where the first confirmed Italian patient was treated had not followed the sanitary protocols. In its own report based on a visit to Italy, the ECDC noted that 'transmission seems to have occurred locally', with health workers and patients having been infected in local hospitals.

By the time the first patients tested positive in Northern Italy, the virus had probably already been around for some time. It was the peak of the annual flu season, which meant the COVID-19 virus was hard to detect. One of the virologists involved in the European PREPARE project, professor Herman Goossens, was convinced that the virus was already present in Italy as early as the second half of January. The problem is that nobody was tested for it at that point.

The high mortality rate and the speed with which the virus spread were remarkable. Some researchers finger-pointed the high levels of air pollution, a major problem in many Northern Italian cities. Others believed that the higher-than-average mortality rate was caused by Italy's ageing population, one of the oldest in the world. Or by Italy's cultural norms: frequent and close interactions between generations, and the traditional hugging and kissing to greet each other. Others still blamed the Champions League football match between Atalanta Bergamo and Valencia, in Milan's San Siro Stadium on 19 February. What could be a better vector than 40,000 hugging fans? According to Dr. Francesco Le Foche, an immunologist at Policlinico Umberto I in Rome, there was indeed an explosion of cases two weeks after the match.

And then there were those who blamed the European Union. Why had Europe not been tougher when all hell broke loose in China?, asked Roberto Burioni, a virologist at Milan's San Raffaele University. At the meeting of health ministers on 13 February, Italy had indeed asked for tougher measures at airports, but Europe had not acted. Burioni was not alone in his 'too little, too late' criticism. The fact that even the former president of the European Parliament, Antonio Tajani, blamed the EU for a lack of coordinated action and for reacting too slowly, showed just how widespread this sentiment was. Whatever the causes, the fact that the hardest hit European country had also been the first to take such bold actions as banning all flights to and from China, made it all the more painful.

A SECOND WAVE IN EUROPE

From Northern Italy, the virus spread like wildfire to other European countries. Neighbouring Croatia got its first confirmed case only a couple of days after Italy's: a Croatian man who had just visited Italy. Same story in Northern Ireland. And in Greece, where a 38-year-old woman tested positive after a visit to Milan. An Italian couple from Lombardy, living in Innsbruck, brought the virus to Austria. And when an Italian doctor and his wife tested positive in Tenerife, the four-star hotel where they were staying was locked down until every tourist and staff member, more than 700 in total, was tested. In mainland Spain, a woman returning to Barcelona from Northern Italy tested positive. France and Germany also reported new cases, all people who had spent some time in the affected Italian regions. By the end of the week eighteen of the 27 EU countries were affected. A football game like the one in San Siro, some après-ski in Ischgl, Austria, and the popular carnival in Germany's Heinsberg, close to the Dutch and Belgian borders, were enough to create clusters of infections.

In that last week of February, the COVID crisis entered a new phase. The priority was no longer on protecting Europe against a viral invasion from China or Asia. The enemy was now within Europe's walls. The EU countries realised that the storm was inevitably coming their way. As the ECDC put it: 'We will likely see similar situations [as in Italy] in other countries in Europe.' The constant stream of dramatic images from Italy spread faster than the virus. The British tabloid *The Sun* quoted an internal memo of the National Security Communications Team, saying that in the worst-case scenario, 80% of Britons could be infected, 'causing up to 500,000 deaths.' That week, the 'killer bug' was on the front page of all newspapers in the UK. In Germany, which then had 27 confirmed cases, health minister Spahn warned that Germany was at the beginning of an epidemic. A crisis team of German health ministers and interior ministers was set up. The next day French president Macron delivered a similar message: 'We are facing a crisis, an epidemic, that is coming' while visiting the Pitié-Salpetrière Hospital in Paris. At that point, the new virus had killed two people in France.

'KEEP THE BORDERS OPEN'

In some countries, populist parties immediately seized the opportunity to link the spread of the virus to Europe's open borders. The leader of the French far-right Rassemblement National Marine Le Pen lashed out at the European Union: 'The only thing [the EU] has done is to condemn those who would consider controlling borders, even temporarily. This proves the strength of the ideology, almost the religion, of borderlessness of the EU leaders.' In Italy, the far-right Lega leader and former interior minister Matteo Salvini felt the same. He jumped on the growing panic to attack the Italian government for not sufficiently protecting Italy's border. The borders should be made 'armour-plated'. He referred to the docking, a couple of days earlier, of the NGO Ocean Viking rescue ship in the Sicilian port of Pozzallo, a ship with 276 African migrants on board. 'Allowing the migrants to land from Africa, where the presence of the virus was confirmed, is irresponsible', Salvini argued. The fact that at that moment there was only one confirmed case in the whole of Africa, in Egypt, seemed to be a mere detail for him. The ship was immediately quarantined and crew members were checked. No one tested positive.

The Italian government did not see any reason to reintroduce border controls, not even temporary checks. On the contrary, it spared no efforts in keeping its borders open and convincing its neighbours to do the same. 'Closing the border would have a devastating impact on the Italian economy', prime minister Conte argued. Italy's efforts paid off. At a meeting in Rome on 25 February, the health ministers of France, Germany, Switzerland, Austria, Slovenia and Croatia promised to keep their borders open. Closing the borders would be 'disproportionate and ineffective', they jointly stated.

The Austrians especially needed to be reassured. In response to the rapidly degrading situation in Northern Italy that weekend, just south of Austria's borders, Austrian interior minister Karl Nehammer pulled together a task force on Sunday morning to discuss whether or not to introduce border controls with Italy. In the evening, Austria stopped a train at the Austrian border, on the Italian side of the Brenner Pass. The train was on its way from Venice to Munich when two passengers showed symptoms of a COVID infection. Only when the two tested negative, was the train allowed to continue, now with a four-hour delay. But at the next day's meeting in Rome, Austria, just like the other ministers who were present, decided to indulge Italy and keep its border open.

This decision was fully in line with the position of the European Commission. When asked for their reaction to the dramatic events in Italy that weekend, European commissioners Janez Lenarčič and Stella Kyriakides, in charge of crisis management and health respectively, acknowledged that imposing border restrictions is up to the EU countries. But at the same time, both commissioners made it very clear that this was not the best option. Any border restriction should be based on a thorough risk assessment and scientific advice. It should be proportionate and above all, it should be coordinated. 'Diverging approaches across the EU should be avoided', commissioner Kyriakides, said at a press conference on 26 February, standing shoulder to shoulder with Italian health minister Roberto Speranza. For Kyriakides, this was 'a test case for EU cooperation'.

COORDINATION DISORDER, AGAIN

Despite all good intentions, there was little cooperation, other than the commitment (for the time being) to keep the borders open. This became clear when EU countries started to issue travel warnings against visiting (part of) Italy or to take special health measures at their airports. Both areas are the responsibility of the countries themselves. They are not obliged to consult each other. The Dutch foreign ministry advised its citizens not to go to the Lombardy region and to be careful when visiting the rest of Italy. Its French counterpart strongly encouraged postponing all non-essential trips to Northern Italy. The German authorities asked citizens to report which places they had visited in Italy as soon as they returned home. Romania decided that people who came from the affected Italian areas would be placed under quarantine for two weeks. The United Kingdom, the Netherlands and France also requested that people coming from outbreak areas in Italy isolate themselves, with or without symptoms. Belgium, on the other hand, did not foresee any specific measures in Brussels Airport.

It wasn't just the EU countries lacking coordination. Even the EU institutions were not aligned. The European Parliament ruled that its employees who had travelled to the affected areas in Italy in the last 14 days should stay home and self-isolate. The European Commission, however, decided on the very same day that its staff members who had visited China or Hong Kong could stay home, but those who had been to Northern Italy should still come to the office to work. The left hand didn't know what the right hand was doing.

Events in Italy and the growing uncertainty in more and more EU countries did not lead to an immediate European policy response. It was, at that point, more of the same. Granted, the Croatian presidency decided on 2 March to upgrade the Integrated Political Crisis Response. Until that point, it was in mode one - mainly being used to exchange information. Now it switched to mode two, which meant more 'roundtables' where ambassadors could compare and coordinate their decisions and actions. The European Commission also geared up a bit and created a 'Corona Response Team'. Five commissioners – the ones covering health, the internal market, mobility, macro-economic policy and crisis management – had to work more closely together. But neither

---

FOCUS ON:

The Integrated Political Crisis Response (IPCR)

The Integrated Political Crisis Response (IPCR) has two modes. Mode one is used to simply exchange information. In mode two, the focus is on coordinating the national emergency response measures of the EU countries. During the COVID-19 crisis it met regularly either at the level of experts or at the level of ambassadors. A wide range of crisis-related topics can be discussed through the IPCR, from repatriation flights to shortages in medical equipment and crisis communication. It is an ad hoc platform that EU countries use to raise urgent and concrete matters that require coordination between the countries and the EU institutions.

---

form of additional support, announced on the same day, had much practical impact. The point was to send the signal that cooperation and solidarity were important. It would soon become clear that this was not enough.

CHAPTER 6

Solidarity Lost

- What solidarity really means in the European Union
- Why European citizens started making their own face masks
- Why the Italian ambassador got so angry

A UNION BUILT ON SOLIDARITY

Solidarity lies at the heart of the European project. Now and then, it's good to go back to the beginning, to the founding texts of the European integration process. The most important one is definitely the Schuman Declaration, presented by the French foreign minister Robert Schuman on 9 May 1950. It is so fundamental that 9 May has been known as 'Europe Day' since 1985. One of the most quoted sentences in that declaration explicitly mentions solidarity: 'Europe will not be made all at once, or according to a single plan. It will be built through concrete achievements which first create a de facto solidarity.'

But what does solidarity really mean in a European context? I see at least three different meanings. In its most idealistic form solidarity is associated with fellowship, with a community of people belonging to a similar group. There is an element of emotion, a moral obligation to stand alongside and help those in the group who need it. When something bad happens to someone in your neighbourhood, the locals roll up their sleeves and do what they can to support each other. In this sense, solidarity is easier to achieve with people that are physically closer to you than with – let's say – the rest of mankind. The stronger the sense of belonging, the greater the solidarity. At the European level, there is no deep common sense of belonging (yet?). 'We have made Italy, now we must make Italians', the Italian painter-politician Massimo d'Azeglio said after Italy's unification in 1861. We might have made Europe, but we haven't yet made Europeans.

In Europe, there are many examples of a second interpretation of solidarity: mutual self-interest. Mutual self-interest is very concrete, very tangible, especially in an emergency. On 22 March, in the midst of the corona crisis no less, a powerful earthquake hit the Croatian capital of Zagreb. Within hours there was a European response. The EU Civil Protection Mechanism (more on that later) was activated. Several countries sent tents, beds, mattresses and heaters to the affected area. This kind of solidarity is like an insurance policy. Every EU country could one day be hit by an earthquake, floods or a terrorist attack, so it's good to know help is at hand. Today it's you, tomorrow it could be me. That is also the logic behind the 'solidarity clause' that was introduced in article 222 of the Lisbon Treaty. This clause makes it easier for EU countries to act together to help out a country that is confronted with a natural or man-made disaster. But even with such rational insurance logic, a sense of belonging helps. Is it a coincidence that the countries closest to Croatia, like Slovenia, Hungary, Austria and Italy, were the first to send aid? Is it a coincidence that the city of Sarajevo, which shares a history with Zagreb, lit up Sarajevo City Hall and sent a message to the mayor of Zagreb that 'Sarajevo does not forget its friends'? Unlikely.

In my opinion, Europe is based mainly on a third type of solidarity. A type that researchers Sofia Fernandes and Eulalia Rubio from the Jacques Delors Institute, inspired by the French sociologist Emile Durkheim, call 'enlightened self-interest'. The self-interest is less tangible at first. EU countries help each other because ultimately, in the end, if others do well and the EU as a whole does well, they will also do well. They believe that they will benefit from the others' success. That's why high-income countries support lower-income countries: if the latter do well, the former have more opportunities to sell their products. 'It is the awareness of being intimately connected and mutually responsible for the preservation of a common project', Fernandes and Rubio argue, 'that has prompted the development of inter-state solidarity arrangements all over the history of European integration.' It is the 'enlightened self-interest' that keeps the European Union in its current state together. When in an important turning point of the euro crisis on 11 February 2010, European leaders promised to take action, they did so not to save Greece, but to save the euro. If Greece imploded, the euro could implode as well.

The same could also be said of the COVID crisis. If the health system of one European country collapsed, or if the disease was not under control in one European country, then the risk that the virus would infect all others or at least the neighbouring countries would increase. Ultimately, no one would be totally safe unless the virus slowed down in the whole of Europe.

In the days immediately following the dramatic outbreak in Italy during the last weekend of February, this insight was missing. The higher the number of infected people, the lower the level of European solidarity. National reflexes prevailed. The lack of solidarity, in all its three forms, was so visible that it even forced the 95-year-old former

Commission president Delors to sound the alarm, something he rarely does. 'The germ is back', he warned. 'The lack of European solidarity poses a mortal danger to the European Union.'

THE FACE MASK TRAGEDY

The most visible sign of this lack of solidarity was a bitter conflict over face masks, a conflict that dominated the first week of March. Only a handful of European countries – the Czech Republic, France, Germany, Poland – produced such masks. When more and more countries all over the world badly needed them, not in the least for their health workers, many EU countries were suddenly confronted with shortages. In some countries, stocks had simply been destroyed, perhaps to save on storage costs. Other countries had decided not to replenish their stocks, like France who had a large stock until 2012.

For European commissioner Janez Lenarčič, the decisive moment came on 28 February when policymakers realised their national stocks were not sufficient. It was the moment when Italy asked to activate the Civil Protection Mechanism but no European country was in favour. That was the moment, the commissioner later said in an interview, that the Commission knew there was a real shortage of protective equipment, not just in Italy, but in most of the EU. 'That was the crunch moment that there is a problem in Europe's ability to face the challenge', he said. That's when reality sank in that the European Union was not fully prepared.

Getting masks was more than challenging. Procurement markets had collapsed or were on the brink. The market no longer functioned properly and deals were not always honoured. In most cases, it was every man for himself. A very telling anecdote was told by the (then) Slovakian prime minister Peter Pellegrini. He told a local TV station that his country had an agreement with Ukraine to buy two million masks. Slovakia would pay cash; a government plane was ready to pick them up. But at the very last moment, a German dealer showed up, paid on the spot and walked off with the supplies. Canadian Prime Minister Justin Trudeau shared a similar anecdote about 'a higher bidder', the US.

Under these conditions, EU countries reacted in one of three ways. Most countries mobilised their citizens and national companies. Several prime ministers and mayors encouraged citizens who were handy with a needle and thread to produce their own face masks at home. 'Face Mask Sewing Tutorials' started popping up online, enthusiastically promoted by one celebrity or another. Famous football teams produced and sold their own masks, complete with club branding of course. In several Belgian prisons, inmates sewed face masks for health workers. In the Czech Republic, students of the Umprum Academy of Arts, Architecture and Design reacted to a Facebook post and used their skills to make masks for one of Prague's maternity hospitals.

National entrepreneurs were equally encouraged to convert their usual production lines. In Italy, the well-known brand of cycling clothing Santini (known for producing the World Champions' rainbow jerseys), started to produce protective face masks. In Spain, the SEAT car company also made ventilators at one of its plants. In Germany, a biofuel company and a brewery developed alcohol-based disinfectants. The French luxury conglomerate LVMH, owner of Louis Vuitton and Dior, also used part of its production facilities to pump out hydroalcoholic gel instead of perfume. The Belgian *jenever* (gin) distillery Filliers did the same. The Commission chipped in by helping companies with guidance on safety standards and on how to put their products on the EU market.

A second way to get your hands on face masks was to try and get them from China. Already before the COVID crisis broke out, China was responsible for around half of the world's production, producing some 20 million masks a day. When the virus began to spread in Wuhan, China expanded its production nearly twelvefold. In their efforts to get access to Chinese deliveries, every government played its own trump card. In Belgium, it was only thanks to the king's intervention with Chinese president Xi Jinping that in mid-March a first delivery of 500,000 masks arrived at Liège Airport. In Germany, the government worked through major companies such as BASF and Lufthansa, which apparently had more leverage with the Chinese government. From Spain to the Czech Republic and Finland, Chinese deliveries or donations were warmly welcomed. Josep Borrell, the EU High Representative for Foreign Affairs and Security Policy (Europe's 'foreign minister') was more critical, however. On 24 March, he warned that there was also 'a geopolitical component' to the COVID-19 crisis, a 'struggle for influence', including through what he called 'the politics of generosity'. It was a clear shot at China.

And then there was a third way, used by those EU countries where face masks were actually produced. They simply kept them for themselves. In the first week of March, the Czech Republic ordered local producers not to export their supplies. Germany also decided to ban the export of personal protection equipment, including face masks. France took a slightly different approach, but with a comparable result. On 3 March, the French government decided to requisition all face mask stocks in the country and to reserve them for patients and health workers in France. This had an immediate impact. Much of the personal protective equipment that was imported from Asia by the Swedish company Mölnlycke was stored in its warehouse in Lyon. The French decision meant that a stock of six million masks was confiscated, which had a knock-on effect on the supply to other EU countries, from Italy and Spain to Belgium and the Netherlands. A French diplomat defended this measure: 'public health was not an EU competence'.

Italy had taken similar measures, but given the dramatic situation in the country, they were broadly forgiven. The same could not be said of the decisions of France and Germany. Members of the European Parliament called for a tough response. For the Greek member of parliament Eva Kaili, such decisions 'ignored the immediate needs of other Member States currently facing extreme emergencies (including Italy), endangering those working in the front line to contain the virus'. Proactive stockpiling of medical equipment should not be allowed, she argued, since this would only make the spread of the pandemic worse. Manfred Weber, the European People's Party leader in the European Parliament, also spoke out against the banning of medical equipment exports, explicitly referring to France and his own country Germany.

CAN THE MINISTERS RESTORE SOLIDARITY?

A large group of smaller EU countries were not amused and put the issue on the agenda of the next extraordinary health ministers Council meeting, on 6 March. Belgian health minister Maggie De Block called the French and German behaviour 'an overreaction' that prevented suppliers from delivering to other countries, even though the necessary contracts had been signed. Dutch, Lithuanian, Estonian and Austrian ministers echoed her message.

But those countries were not left high and dry. They got the support of the European Commission, which is there to guard the broader European interest. Commissioner

Janez Lenarčič called it non-European to close oneself within one national market. He feared that such measures would prevent essential equipment from reaching the people who needed it most. His appeal was supported by the WHO's European director, the Belgian Hans Kluge who called this 'a test for European solidarity and leadership'. An only-for-me response when an all-for-one-spirit was needed, Commission president Ursula von der Leyen called it later that month.

France and Germany went to great lengths to explain their decisions. Both health ministers asked their colleagues for understanding. Their countries were harder hit than others, so they needed more protective equipment than others (a questionable argument). Waiting for the group purchase that the Commission had launched in February was not an option: the procedures were simply too slow and too bureaucratic. They appreciated the fact that commissioner Thierry Breton, in charge of the internal market, was talking with the industry to rapidly produce more masks, but it was all too little too late. In the meantime, governments had to protect their people, the ministers argued.

Especially the German health minister Spahn took his time to explain the measure. Don't call it an 'export ban', he said. Given the huge global demand, Germany simply wanted to avoid an international bidding war and instead get the face masks to the countries that needed them the most. Other EU countries would still receive face masks and gloves, if they asked for them. Spahn tried to reassure his colleagues: 'If it is for a European neighbour country, it is more likely that we are going to say yes'.

At the end of the health ministers Council meeting both countries, however, gave no indication that they would withdraw their national measures any time soon. On the contrary, the French and German ministers even asked the Croatian presidency not to focus too much on this sensitive and divisive issue in the conclusions of the meeting. But the presidency, pressured by the Commission and the smaller EU countries, insisted on having more European cooperation in this area. The availability of medical equipment and medicines had to be monitored on the European level, 'with the aim of securing the production, stocking, availability and rational use of protective equipment in the Union.' In the end, the French and German restrictive measures were only abandoned after heavy pressure from the European Commission and the worst-affected countries.

At the 6 March meeting, solidarity was at an all-time low. Lofty words like solidarity and cooperation jarred with the reality on the ground. Just like during the 2009 health crisis, when the priority of the EU countries was to secure vaccines for their own citizens. And just like the first phase of the 2010 banking crisis, when they tried to save their own banks. Until they realised that their banks were so closely intertwined with other European banks that a European solution was the only real solution.

Italy, in particular, considered the whole thing a slap in the face. Its doctors and nurses were fighting a war without being properly armed. In the first month of the outbreak, at least 2300 Italian health workers were infected. By the end of March, more than sixty doctors had died. For many Italians this was the third time in a decade that Europe had let them down. First during the 2009 sovereign debt crisis, then during the refugee crisis, and now – again – during the COVID-19 crisis.

Four days after the ministers' meeting, the Italian ambassador to the European Union, Maurizio Massari, wrote an op-ed in which he bluntly criticised the EU's lack of solidarity. The main theme was 'selfishness': 'This is a battle', he wrote, 'in which we are facing two terrible enemies: panic and selfishness (…) The virus will pass, but any rotten seeds of complacency or selfishness will stay'. The ambassador also asked for concrete measures: 'It's time now for the EU to go beyond engagement and consultations, with emergency actions that are quick, concrete and effective.'

The underlying tone was one of disappointment, even bitterness. Italy had asked to activate the European Union Mechanism of Civil Protection, asking mainly for protective equipment such as face masks. But not a single EU country responded to the call. While Italians were dying, others were stockpiling. A bitter pill for those who believed in European solidarity. It also shone a new light on the well-intended decision taken by France, Germany and the United Kingdom a week earlier, to send emergency medical equipment to Iran.

The irony went from bad to worse. There were two countries that did respond positively to Italy's cry for help: Russia, which sent material that turned out to be of very low quality, and China. After a phone call between the Italian foreign minister Luigi Di Maio and his Chinese counterpart Wang Yi, the Chinese promised to deliver over two million face masks and some 10,000 ventilators. When on 13 March the first plane arrived with nine doctors and nine pallets of medical equipment, Di Maio made sure that everybody knew where the help came from. Di Maio posted a video message on his Facebook page, with a clear message: 'Many foreign ministers offered their solidarity and want to give us a hand ... and this evening I wanted to show you the first aid arrived from China.' He went on: 'This is what we call solidarity and I am sure more will come. We are not alone, there are people in the world who want to help Italy'. Painful.

CHAPTER 7

A Dramatic Turn

- When a topic is suddenly considered 'Chefsache' in Europe
- Why European leaders got involved on 10 March
- How prime ministers and presidents can change course

CHEFSACHE, AN ELUSIVE CONCEPT

One of the most intriguing words in European politics is Chefsache. The word was introduced into German politics by former chancellor Gerhard Schröder in the late 1990s. It was used to indicate that he, and not his minister(s), would deal with a particular issue. From there it found its way into the European vocabulary. How it works, and just how powerful it is, became clear to me during the financial crisis in Cyprus, when I was working for the European Council. In 2013 Cyprus hit troubled waters. The country's banking sector was strongly affected by the Greek debt crisis. When its second largest bank, the Laiki Bank, was no longer able to attract private money, the government had to step in. But the burden was too big to carry. By March Cyprus was on the brink of collapse, financially but also politically. The country desperately needed a European aid package.
The discussions on this package were in the hands of the

eurozone finance ministers, the then 17 countries that used the euro as their currency. But an agreement on a ten billion euro rescue package between them and the Cypriot government proved more difficult than expected. When they finally did agree, it was rejected by the parliament of Cyprus. The fact that ordinary bank depositors had to foot part of the bill to rescue the banks created a public outcry. Chaos was rife, the crisis risked boiling over, and the reaction of the markets could push the island completely over the edge. Something had to be done.

That's when chancellor Angela Merkel and European Council president Van Rompuy agreed that the topic would become 'Chefsache': the leaders (the 'Chefs') would now deal with it. The weekend of 22-24 March, Van Rompuy organised an emergency meeting in Brussels, at the highest political level, with the newly elected president of Cyprus and the three presidents of the Commission, the European Central Bank and the Eurogroup. After 12 hours of intense negotiations, worth a book of its own, the leaders reached an agreement just before midnight on Sunday night. And just before the markets in Asia opened. On Monday it was formalised by the finance ministers. This was how fast Chefsache could work.

FOCUS ON:

The European Council

Unlike the Council, which brings together ministers of the 27 EU countries, the European Council brings together their leaders. For most countries this is the prime minister, for a handful the president (e.g. France) and for two, Austria and Germany the chancellor. Since the Lisbon Treaty, the European Council has a president that is nominated for five years. The current president is former Belgian prime minister Charles Michel.

When and why an issue becomes Chefsache – in other words, when and why the heads of state or government get involved – is not explicitly mentioned in the European Treaty. The Treaty itself is actually very general when it comes to the role of the European Council: to 'provide the necessary impetus for the development of the European Union and set out the general political guidelines.' This suggests that the European Council mainly deals with broad high-level strategies on Europe's future. And that is definitely part of what the European Council does. For example, after the last European elections in 2019, the leaders adopted a new strategic agenda which listed Europe's main priorities for the coming five years.

But adopting such high-level strategies is by far not its most important job. Over the years, the European Council has developed into the main crisis manager within the EU system, as the Cypriot banking crisis showed. Instead of meeting three times a year, as was the case in the 1990s, it now meets as often as needed, even on an ad hoc basis when there is an emergency. When a topic is stuck at the level of ministers, when it has several dimensions that go beyond the remit of one specific minister, and is politically very sensitive, then it can move up to the European Council. If and when that happens is decided by its president, usually in close consultation with at least some EU countries. A good example of an issue that the leaders took under their wing is the Economic and Monetary Union. The European multiannual budget of the EU is another one, as is climate change. For years, climate change was discussed by the environment ministers. But when, in preparation for the 2015 Paris climate conference, very tough decisions had to be made, decisions which had an impact on fiscal, transport, energy, agricultural and industrial policies, it shifted to the leaders and became Chefsache.

COVID-19 FOR LEADERS

On 10 March, COVID-19 became Chefsache. Until then, the COVID-19 outbreak had mainly been discussed at a technical level by the health experts, or at the ambassadors' level in COREPER. The ministers had also discussed it a couple of times. European Council president Charles Michel was not personally involved yet, but his cabinet were closely following all the discussions. The same goes for European Commission president Ursula von der Leyen. Within the Commission, the topic was mainly the responsibility of the commissioners in the Commission's Corona team, not of the president.

In the early days of March, von der Leyen and Michel's attention was mainly focused on another threat: the Syrian conflict and the situation at the Greek-Turkish border. In late February, fighting between Syrian rebels supported by Turkey and Syrian government forces backed by Russian air power had escalated. In one attack, 33 Turkish soldiers had lost their lives. The heavy fighting also worsened the already dramatic humanitarian situation in the province of Idlib, sending a new wave of around one million refugees towards the Turkish-Syrian border. Turkish president Erdoğan, dissatisfied with the assistance he got from the EU, threatened to open the Turkish borders with Greece and Bulgaria. Before long, thousands of migrants had gathered in the no man's land between Turkey and Greece. Day after day, pressure on the Greek border police and military troops increased. The number of ships patrolling the seas around the Aegean islands and the number of troops sent by Greece, but also by Bulgaria, sharply increased.

The ghost of the refugee crisis that shook the Union to its core in 2015 had arrived. On 3 March, the presidents of the European Council, the European Commission and the European Parliament jointly paid a visit to the

Greek-Turkish border. Later, this was seen by some commentators as proof that the EU leadership had neglected the COVID-19 crisis, blindsided as they were by those problems. The reality is more nuanced. Given the huge impact of the migration crisis in previous years, it was to be expected that leaders at the highest level would take the events at Europe's border seriously. With hindsight, one could argue that they should have divided their attention, instead of leaving the COVID-19 crisis in the hands of the ministers and commissioners alone.

But after the divisive and inconclusive meeting of the health ministers on 6 March, pressure grew on the leaders to roll up their sleeves. The exponentially rising number of infections and deaths, the clear lack of solidarity between EU countries and the outspoken Italian criticism spilled over the boundaries of health policy. Some countries started to seriously think about unilateral border restrictions, which would affect the European single market. And to make things worse, the markets got more and more upset. On Monday 9 March, the global stock markets suffered their worst day since the global financial crisis of 2008. In one day, hundreds of billions of dollars, euros and pounds were wiped off stocks across the world. Some European markets plunged by around 8%. The same day, the Italian government put the entire country, 60 million people, and the third biggest economy of Europe, on complete lockdown. Without warning.

On that same Monday morning, Commission president von der Leyen looked back at her first 100 days in office. Her main message was that the Commission's long-term agenda – the Green Deal, the Digital Agenda, a stronger Europe in the world – was very much on track. She also focused at length on the one topic that had kept her and president Michel busy for the past days: defusing the crisis with Turkey and the tension at the Greek-Turkish border.

That evening both leaders would meet Turkish president Erdoğan in Brussels to discuss this. Von der Leyen mentioned the COVID crisis, but only briefly: it was in the capable hands of her team of commissioners, which met 'on a weekly basis'. The word 'weekly' was probably not the best choice, given the speed at which the virus was overwhelming the European continent.

The next day, on the request of the French president and others, Charles Michel scheduled a videoconference of European leaders. Preparation time had been very short, so the results of the almost three-hour call were not very concrete or detailed. The meeting taking place was the main message. By discussing the unfolding crisis at their level, the leaders sent a signal that they would not leave this crisis in the hands of their ministers and experts alone. They, the European leaders, were ready to step in. They wanted to weigh in on two fronts: better coordinating all actions to contain the virus, and stabilising the economy. That the leaders were very concerned about the economic impact of the COVID-19 crisis explained why European Central Bank president Christine Lagarde and Eurogroup president Mário Centeno also participated in the talks.

FOCUS ON:

The European Commission

The European Commission has the 'right of initiative': it is in principle the only European institution that has the power to propose legislation. It is on the basis of the Commission's proposal that the Council of Ministers and the European Parliament will try to find an agreement. This gives the Commission a powerful position. It also makes sure that the legislation and the Treaties are followed, and manages most of the EU's budget. Every EU country has a commissioner. Together they employee 32,000 civil servants. Since December 2019, the Commission's president is Ursula von der Leyen.

ENOUGH HOMEWORK FOR EVERYONE

The meeting resulted in a series of tasks. There was enough work to go around. To cushion the economic impact, Europe needed a plan to inject some 25 billion euros into national health care systems, small businesses and badly hit economic sectors. The Commission took the lead. 'We will use all the tools at our disposal to make sure that the European economy weathers this storm', von der Leyen said after the meeting. The Commission would explore if money from the European budget that had not yet been used could be redirected. It would also see what more could be done, together with the finance ministers, to help national governments. It could take a look at the state aid rules and the Stability and Growth Pact, two frameworks that prescribed how and when governments could spend money. Perhaps a bit more flexibility in the application of those rules would allow countries to spend more. Christine Lagarde also confirmed that the European Central Bank was ready to muck in.

The health ministers and interior ministers also got some homework. Almost every day now, governments were taking decisions to control the virus without informing each other. Some countries like Denmark, the Netherlands, Slovenia and Ireland had banned all gatherings of more than 100 people. In the Czech Republic an event could not have more than 30 guests. In Finland and Sweden, 500 attendees was the threshold. In France, Greece and Belgium, 1000 was the limit.

This is just one example of how Europe was becoming a patchwork of uncoordinated decisions. But there were many more. In France, you could no longer visit grandparents in a care home, in other countries you could. Belgium kept its nurseries open, other countries didn't. In Poland, you could still go to church, in Belgium all religious services were cancelled. Of course, not all measures should be decided at the European level. Some of them are better handled at the national or even the regional level. To be fair, several countries, especially larger, decentralised ones in which the main responsibility for health policy was in the hands of local authorities, turned into a patchwork of measures. But some of these measures did have an impact on neighbouring countries, especially in border regions. That's why the health and interior ministers were asked to coordinate more regularly, ideally on a daily basis, under the leadership of the Commission.

And then there was the difficult issue of shortages in protective equipment. How much material was available in the EU, and how much was needed? How could face masks be better distributed to where they were most needed? And how to get rid of the export bans on medical equipment? The leaders asked the Commission to work on a solution.

The first videoconference of European leaders was very much the warm-up. Now the real work could start. But perhaps even more important at that moment than these practical decisions was to get Italy back on side. In a separate videoconference with the Italian prime minister Conte, the day after the European Council meeting, the Commission and Italy aligned their positions and issued a joint statement. The Commission reiterated its wish that all restrictive measure put in place by an EU country would first be discussed at the European level, so that vital supplies would go where they are needed most. (Ironically, Romania announced that same day that it would also ban exports of medicines and medical equipment).

Von der Leyen also had a more personal message for the people of Italy. In a video message in Italian she reassured them: 'Dear Italians, at this difficult moment, I would like to tell all of us fighting against the virus that you are not alone. (…) Europe suffers with Italy (…) Rest assured that this family, your family, will not leave you on your own.' A message echoed by Angela Merkel in a press conference the same day: Germany will help Italy 'in a way friends help friends'. A couple of days later, Germany announced that it would send 1 million face masks to Italy.

The 10 March videoconference, though low on concrete results, was a first important turning point. In the days that followed, several EU country leaders made a point of showing that they were in charge. By then the World Health Organization had also declared COVID-19 a pandemic, with 'alarming levels of spread and severity'. Such an announcement did not change much in practice, but did more in terms of perception. On 12 March, president Macron addressed the French nation, warning of 'the worst health crisis that France had known in a century'. He explicitly called for a 'European response'. In an effort to calm the financial markets, he shared his belief that European governments would support the European economy, 'quoi qu'il en coûte', whatever the cost. The speech he gave to the nation four days later was even more solemn. 'France is at war', he repeated six times to the more than 35 million viewers, an absolute record in the history of French television. 96.1% of all people watching TV at that moment heard the president announce tough, never-before-seen measures. Even the second round of the local elections was cancelled, something that four days before was not yet considered necessary.

Other speeches were equally dramatic in tone. In Spain, after a seven-hour meeting with his ministers, prime minister Sanchez spoke to the Spanish population. He announced a state of emergency. 'We will have at our disposal the armed forces – the army is prepared for this', Sanchez said. In the Netherlands, the address to the nation by prime minister Rutte on 16 March was equally historic. It was the first time that a Dutch prime minister had spoken to the nation on TV and radio since 1973, when then prime minister Joop den Uyl announced a series of difficult messages following the Arab oil boycott and its resulting economic crisis. In Belgium, King Filip also spoke to the nation, something a Belgian king usually only does at Christmas and on the Belgian national holiday. In Germany, Angela Merkel's speech was equally unprecedented. 'Since German unification, no, since World War II, there has been no greater challenge to our country that depends so much on us acting together in solidarity', Merkel said in what was her first national televised address since she became German Chancellor in 2005, apart from her annual New Year's Eve speeches. There could be no doubt: in the days following 10 March, leaders joined the fight against the virus. From then on, COVID-19 was Chefsache. Things started to move.

PART 2

SAVING UNITY,
SAVING THE UNION

The very first COVID-19 meeting of the European leaders on 10 March did not solve all the problems. But at least it mobilised the highest political level. The meeting clearly outlined what had to be done. First, solidarity had to be restored, especially with Italy. This was crucial, not least for perception, and therefore made its way to the top of the to-do list. Second, the single market had to be preserved. This was necessary not only to make sure that medical equipment could reach its destination, but also to avoid shortages of other goods within the EU.

Restoring solidarity and preserving the single market were two goals that could be achieved relatively quickly. The third, safeguarding the free movement of people, would take a bit longer. The intentions of some EU countries to reinstall border controls became apparent in the second week of March. If they were going to take that step, the process should at least be properly managed. The fourth objective was probably even more complex: how to handle the socio-economic impact of the COVID-19 crisis. The fact that all relevant players participated in the meeting on 10 March – not only the 27 EU heads of state but also the European Commission, European Central Bank, Eurogroup and the High Representative for Foreign Policy – was crucial to get the ball rolling. Work on short-term emergency measures could start. This is the core of part 2 of this book.

CHAPTER 8

Solidarity Restored

- How the EU could react faster to emergency situations
- How Europe brought its stranded citizens back home
- Why the EU needs its own stocks of medical equipment

'Member states expressed sympathy with Italy and other member states that are severely hit'. This first sentence of the summary of the 10 March European Council video meeting illustrates how important it was for Europe's leaders to restore solidarity.

This could be done by using Europe's health emergency mechanisms. When it comes to crisis response, the ball is firmly in the court of the EU countries. If a country is hit by a devastating earthquake or catastrophic flooding, it is up to each and every country within the EU to decide whether it wants to take part in an EU emergency mechanism. Based on the response, the Commission can then start to coordinate.

For the COVID-19 outbreak specifically, there were two mechanisms that countries could use to address critical medical shortages: joint public procurements and the Union Civil Protection Mechanism.

One of the lessons learnt after the outbreak of the H1N1 pandemic in 2009 was that not all EU countries are in a position to get vaccines on time or at an affordable price. A possible solution is that countries join forces and buy these vaccines together through so-called joint public procurements. The result is not only that participating countries get a better price, but that they are also guaranteed to get at least part of the stock that was collectively bought. When a country goes on a lone shopping expedition, this is not always guaranteed. Joint public procurements became possible for vaccines and medicines in 2010. In 2013 the scope of these public procurements was broadened to also include medical equipment, which came in quite handy when the COVID-19 crisis hit. Soon after the crisis broke out, several countries expressed interest in a group purchase. Almost all EU countries participated in at least one of four joint procurement initiatives (each one had around 20 participating countries) to buy a wide variety of products, from laboratory equipment to face masks and face shields. The most popular initiative, in which 26 countries participated, was to buy ventilators, machines that breath for you when your lungs fail. It would appear that no country wanted to end up in the same situation as Italy, where serious shortages forced doctors to choose whose life should be saved and whose not.

But the procedures were painfully slow. Between the launch and the actual signing of the contracts, there were several weeks of negotiations. The real problem was the delivery time, which ranged from a couple of weeks to, in one case, more than fifty weeks. The problem was of course the market. Global demand was high, all countries worldwide needed huge amounts of medical equipment, producers couldn't keep up. Causing even more confusion, individual EU countries had simultaneously launched their own national procurement initiatives, in parallel to the European ones. The race was on. But there were no winners as most of the material arrived way too late for the first COVID peak.

A second emergency response mechanism that was activated during the COVID crisis was the Union Civil Protection Mechanism (UCPM). Any country, from the EU or not, that is hit by a disaster too big to be handled alone can ask the EU and six other participating countries for help. The affected country tells the Commission what it needs, from field hospitals to medicines, and the Commission then pools and coordinates all the donated help. Since its creation in 2001 this mechanism has been used in more than 300 emergencies, including the 2015 earthquake in Nepal and the 2018 Ebola outbreak in the Democratic Republic of the Congo.

In the COVID crisis the UCPM played an important role. Most of the requests related to emergency medical equipment or medical personnel. Initially, this got off to a very bad start. One of the first countries to call on the UCPM, in late February, was Italy. Commissioner Janez Lenarčič welcomed the request for help: 'Italy is part of

FOCUS ON:

The Union Civil Protection Mechanism (UCPM)

Besides the 27 EU countries, six other countries participate in the Union Civil Protection Mechanism: Iceland, Norway, Serbia, North Macedonia, Montenegro and Turkey. The UK participates during the Brexit transition period. Through the UCPM, the Commission contributes to at least 75% of the costs. Recent aid operations include the forest fires in Sweden, Bolivia and Greece in 2018 and 2019. During the COVID-19 crisis, more than forty requests were made, including seven from EU countries.

our European family and we will do all we can to help. (…)
All countries should show solidarity.' But this was wishful
thinking. There was no solidarity during the first week of
March. Italy's cry for help remained unanswered for a very
long time. The lack of response, coupled with France and
Germany's export bans on medical equipment which were
announced in the same week, painted a picture of a 'union'
of countries unwilling to help each other out.

Without EU countries offering to help, the UCPM is
pretty much an empty shell. The reason for this is that
there is no common stockpile of medical material that is
managed at the EU level and that can be rapidly deployed
to places in need. So in its current set-up, the UCPM is
more of a facilitator that depends very much on what the
countries decide to offer, if anything.

Within the UCPM, there was, however, one tool that
could be put to use: RescEU. RescEU was still pretty new,
barely one year old. One of the reasons why RescEU was
created was the following one: climate change means
that there is a real risk that extreme disasters such as
floods and forest fires would hit several countries at the
same time. When several countries need their planes and
helicopters to fight fires in their own countries, they cannot
make them available under the UCPM. They just can't be in
two places at once.

That's where RescEU comes in. It is in fact a kind of European reserve of material that, when things are fine, is either
owned, rented or leased by individual countries. When
trouble hits, though, the EU gets first dibs. In return for being prepared to make this material available to the EU, the
countries get EU financing. The point is that the EU could
always rely on sufficient material in case of an emergency,
independent of the additional voluntary offers that may
(or may not) be made by the countries. To make sure that
the materials would go where they are most needed, deci-

sions on deployment would be taken by the Commission. When RescEU was created, it consisted mainly of fire-fighting planes and helicopters. But on 19 March, because of the COVID-19 crisis, the reserve was expanded to also include personal protection equipment, ventilators, laboratory supplies and (in the future) vaccines. Around €370 million was made available to pay for this stockpile of medical equipment. While the arrangement still very much depended on contributions from the countries, this first ever common European stock of medical equipment is nevertheless a step towards a more European, more centralised emergency response. The real sting in the tail of course is that, had it included face masks before the crisis, the Commission could have come to Italy's rescue.

Despite the very difficult start in using the UCPM, by the beginning of April assistance (finally) started to flow throughout Europe, including to Italy. Romania sent a fifteen-strong medical team of doctors and nurses, Austria sent 1.5 million face masks and more than 3300 litres of disinfectant to its southern neighbour. Commission president von der Leyen reached a deal with China for the delivery of more than two million face masks, which the EU then sent to Italy.

France and Germany had also had a change of heart and donated one million masks and seven tons of masks respectively to Italy. An op-ed by the German finance and foreign ministers on 6 April, also published in an Italian and a Spanish newspaper, almost sounded like a mea culpa: 'One of the truths of this terrifying pandemic is that Europe was not at first adequately prepared (…) We need a clear expression of European solidarity in the corona pandemic. Germany is willing'. To confirm its commitment, Germany made intensive care beds available to more than 200 infected patients from France and Italy, and sent a team of doctors to Spain. The image of a self-ish Europe that we saw in the first week of March had, by the first week of April, been replaced by a perception of a more caring one.

It wasn't just the French patients being airlifted to Lux-embourg or the Polish doctors working in the hard-hit city of Bergamo that made European solidarity very vis-ible. EU countries were also working together to bring back home the more than 625,000 European citizens stranded abroad. More and more commercial airlines had stopped flying and more and more countries world-wide were closing their air space. For many Europeans the only way to get home was to call the local embassies or the crisis centres set up by the foreign ministries, in the hope that they would send a repatriation flight. Here again, joining forces was a no-brainer. Instead of Lith-uania, Belgium or Spain each sending a whole plane to pick up just ten Lithuanians, fifteen Belgians and thirty Spaniards respectively, cooperation at the EU level made much more sense.

The UCPM also had a role to play here. When a country organised a repatriation flight, the EU covered part of the cost if other EU citizens were allowed on board too. From late January, when France asked to activate the UCPM to repatriate 64 French and 135 EU citizens on a flight they arranged from Wuhan, around eighty thousand Europeans got home on one of the 350 flights facilitated and co-financed by the UCPM. Thanks to this financial incentive, around 30% of passengers that were brought back had a different nationality than the country that or-ganised the flight. This too was solidarity in action.

The picture I paint is definitely too rosy for insiders. Of course, I have heard the stories of diplomats in far-flung embassies who had to fight with overzealous counter-parts, everyone trying to get their own people on a flight first; of places where European coordination was difficult or even non-existent; of the families that desperately tried to get on a flight, but did not make it; of the guys in the national crisis centre trying desperately to interpret the funding rules for their UCPM flights; of a national civil servant who had pinned his hopes on the joint public procurement procedure getting his country the test kits it needed...

And I definitely remember the reactions of my Italian friends and colleagues: 'Where was Europe when we needed you?' But after the initial shock and the first moments of shooting from the hip, solidarity was restored and ways were found to deal with the many practical problems. It reminded me of the previous big crisis, the euro and banking crisis. Initially, EU countries tried to save their own banks, the money of their own citizens. Until the leaders realised and accepted, at their landmark meeting in Brussels' Solvay Library on 11 February 2010, that economic and financial stability was a 'shared responsibility'. It seems that in every crisis, the EU first needs a meta-crisis, a clash of hurt feelings, before solidarity kicks in.

CHAPTER 9

The Single Market Preserved

- Why the single market is so important for Europe
- Why Serbia called European solidarity a fairy tale
- Why the shelves in the shops were never empty

In their videoconference of 10 March, European leaders stressed one form of solidarity in particular: medical equipment should be delivered to where it was most needed. To achieve that, the single market should function properly. Without 'unjustified obstacles', European Council president Michel concluded, naming no names, but clearly referring to the German and French export restrictions. The word 'unjustified' is key. After all, is it really unjustified to 'put on your own mask before helping others with theirs'? In other words, first making sure your own citizens and health workers are protected before thinking about the needs of health workers in other countries? An easy question from a European perspective, but not necessarily for politicians whose careers depend on national voters.

Legally, in this particular situation, a case could perhaps be made for export restrictions. As a general rule, the European Treaty does not allow countries to prohibit or restrict exports to other EU countries. Fortunately, because without that rule, the single market wouldn't exist. If a European company makes a product that requires components from other countries, then it can be certain that it will get those. But the European Treaty also foresees a limited number of exceptions to that rule. Protecting health is one of them. The Commission, however, looked at the French and German export restrictions not from a national, but from a European perspective. According to the Commission, national export restrictions were only possible if they did not aggravate shortages throughout the EU. Preventing shortages in your own country while creating shortages in other countries with acute needs went against the spirit of European cooperation. For the Commission it was a matter of principle: to preserve the idea of European solidarity, but also to protect the single market.

When it comes to protecting the single market, the Commission has a lot of power. It has the authority to intervene if a country obstructs the free flow of goods and services within the EU, and it does not shy away from using legal action whenever that happens. Also in this case, the Commission made it clear that if the countries in question did not drop their export restrictions, there could be financial penalties: the borders simply had to remain open for goods.

FOCUS ON:

The single market

In 2018, the single market accounted on average for two thirds of all the exports of the individual EU countries. It is by far the most important source of economic growth. In the context of the COVID-19 crisis, a special task force was set up to discuss any obstacles that hindered the free movement of goods and services, the Single Market Enforcement Task Force. It got underway on 8 April.

The Commission also made use of its powers in another area, trade. One reason that France and Germany had given to justify their export restrictions was to prevent companies from selling medical material to players outside the European Union. That could be fixed, the Commission reasoned. There was not so much a need for national export restrictions, but for European ones. On 15 March, a Sunday, the Commission made a decision: manufacturers or distributors of certain categories of medical products, such as face masks, gloves or protective goggles, could only export these goods outside the EU if they got a green light from their government. Before giving that green light, the government in question had to consult the other EU countries to make sure they did not have shortages. The EU was quick to say that its European solution was not the same as an export ban: the arrangement still allowed humanitarian aid to other countries in the world that needed help. But other than that, the priority was to make sure that there were no major shortages in the EU itself. At least that Franco-German argument was off the table.

This 'EU first' approach was not much appreciated by outsiders. 'European solidarity, that's a fairy tale', the Serbian president Vučić concluded when he heard the news. Close partners like Switzerland and Norway were not amused either. The reactions caused some tweaks to be made to the arrangement. It was reduced to only cover protective masks, and neighbouring countries were exempt from the export restrictions. In other words, exporting to these countries would work in the same way as exporting to any EU country. Not including the partners had clearly been a mistake that had to be corrected.

Within the EU, the European export restrictions did the trick. On the very same day that they came into effect, internal market commissioner Thierry Breton tweeted, with some relief and slightly triumphant: 'After intense discussions, I welcome that Germany and France now allow for export of #COVID19 protective equipment. No single European country can win this battle alone.' Still trying to smooth things over with the Italians, he also tweeted it in Italian.

A few days later, Germany officially withdrew its export ban. The others followed. But on the ground it took some time before all the problems were solved. One dispute that got quite some media attention in early April was between France and Sweden. Because of the French export ban, face masks produced for Italy and Spain by the Swedish company Mölnlycke were stuck in a warehouse in Lyon, France. It took many weeks and a phone call from the Swedish prime minister to the French president and prime minister before France lifted the ban. 'We are very pleased to now be able to deliver the facemasks to healthcare professionals in Spain and Italy where they are greatly needed', the CEO of Mölnlycke said diplomatically on 4 April.

The free flow of much-needed face masks and other medical equipment was important to show that there was indeed solidarity with the EU. But it was equally important that other goods and services continued to flow as well. Can you imagine what would happen if shops ran out of food, cosmetics, toiletries and toilet paper, a product apparently in particularly high demand in some countries? All these goods had to reach their destinations quickly and easily. Even when countries reinstalled border checks. If not, people would soon lose trust in the single market.

Commission president Ursula von der Leyen therefore invited all countries to designate so-called 'green lanes'. In these 'green lanes' trucks should be able to cross the border in less than 15 minutes. Time is money, even more so for trucks carrying perishable goods. Some form of ID, a driver's license or at most a letter from their employer should be enough for truck drivers to pass the border, the Commission suggested. Health checks at border points should only take place once, not on each side of the border, and should be organised in the most efficient way. Ideally, the truck driver should not leave their cabin for the check. Small measures, but effective: the waiting time at most border crossings decreased dramatically. At several border crossings, technical problems would continue to pop up throughout the crisis. These would be discussed on a case by case basis between the Commission and the countries involved. But by early April, the fundamental issues that had been affecting the single market were solved. As the European Council had asked.

CHAPTER 10

Saving Schengen

- How the Schengen countries reacted to COVID-19
- Why one country after another 'closed' its borders
- How the 2020 summer holidays were saved (sort of)

In the summer of 1990, I travelled around Europe with an Interrail pass. Different trains of all shapes, sizes and colours took me through eight different countries. If I were to make the same trip again today, with Czechoslovakia and Yugoslavia having been dissolved, I would cross ten borders instead of eight. But crossing ten borders now would be much quicker and easier than crossing eight back then. One reason: Schengen.

Recently, I Googled some pictures of the signing ceremony of the Schengen Agreement, which took place on 14 June 1985. A picture really does speak a thousand words. No solemn atmosphere, nobody aware of the gravitas of that moment. Just thirteen people crammed like sardines into a tiny room, some of them sitting down, others standing up in no apparent logical order or choreography. Two of the participants are enjoying a private joke, one holds up a traffic sign with the words 'ZOLL/DOUANE' (customs) crossed out. There are no prime ministers in the picture, not even a minister. It was the secretaries of state that the three Benelux countries, France and Germany sent to the signing ceremony aboard the MS Princess Marie-Astrid pleasure cruiser on the Moselle River. The nearby village of Schengen, a small village of around 500 inhabitants, had a highly symbolic location, at the meeting point of Luxembourg, France and Germany. But expectations were low. The five countries that signed the treaty – the five other members of the European Economic Community at that time were not interested – agreed to abolish their internal borders, but they were not sure whether this would ever work. It was an experiment.

These signatures paved the way for one of Europe's biggest success stories. But there were teething problems. It would be ten years before the borders between the Schengen countries were dismantled. Now, 35 years later, we have a Schengen Area. Within it, over 400 million Europeans and hundreds of thousands of non-European tourists or business people can move around freely without having to show a passport.

The good thing about Schengen is that it makes the benefits of European cooperation very visible for European citizens. No long queues at border crossings, smooth procedures at the airport. Less visible, but no less important, are the economic benefits. One study produced by the

FOCUS ON:

The Schengen Area

Schengen is an area without internal borders, composed of 26 countries: 22 of the 27 EU countries, Norway, Switzerland, Iceland and Lichtenstein, which was the last to join in 2011. Ireland is out, Bulgaria, Romania, Cyprus and Croatia are on their way in.

Jacques Delors Institute and the Bertelsmann Foundation estimated the economic cost if Schengen would not exist at €63 billion a year. A rather detailed study ordered by the European Parliament predicts a loss of €100-230 billion over 10 years if Schengen were dismantled. And the 2016 French study 'The Economic Costs of Rolling Back Schengen' concluded that if we gave up Schengen, trade between Schengen countries would in the long run fall by 10% to 20%. The Schengen Area's GDP would be reduced by more than €100 billion. Each study comes up with different numbers, depending on how they measure the impact exactly, but the main message is always the same: the economic benefits of not having permanent borders controls are huge.

It doesn't hurt now and again to remind ourselves of the benefits of the Schengen Area, especially since the focus in recent years has been on its weaknesses (and quite rightly so). The fact that several of the terrorists involved in the deadly attacks in Paris in November 2015 and in Brussels in March 2016 could move unhindered and unnoticed between Syria, Belgium and France showed serious risks in the Schengen system. In the same period, Europe was confronted with an influx of refugees and migrants. In 2015 alone more than 1.2 million people requested asylum in Europe, more than double compared to the previous year (but still much less than in countries like Lebanon and Turkey). Public opinion was starting to bubble up.

Schengen is based on rules, but even more on trust. The trust that all countries will effectively protect Europe's external borders. When it started to look like Europe had sprung a leak or two, that trust evaporated. National governments started to take back control of their own internal borders. Germany was first, in September 2015. Others – Austria, Slovenia, Hungary, Sweden, Norway, Denmark and Belgium – followed. France did the same after the November terrorist attacks in Paris, which killed 130 people. In a matter of months, Schengen seemed to have become a thorn in the side of Europe. In 2016 and 2017, many observers predicted the complete collapse of the Schengen Area. Its obituaries were already being written. The reality was, as always, more nuanced. The majority of Schengen members did not return to border controls. In the countries that did, it wasn't necessarily a case of checks along their entire border. Germany, for instance, was tough on its border with Austria, through which large groups of illegal migrants had entered, but way more relaxed with the Netherlands. The overall picture, though, was not pretty. The fact that Slovenia actually built a fence at its border with another Schengen member (Italy) and a future Schengen member (Croatia) was at odds with the concept of a border-free continent. For far-right populist parties this was *gefundenes Fressen*. Schengen was at risk unless the EU could build up a stronger asylum and migration system, and better protect its external borders.

STOPPING A VIRUS WITH BORDER CONTROLS?

Work on this was ongoing, albeit painfully slow, when the COVID-19 virus crossed Europe's external borders. One of the weapons countries deployed to fight the virus, akin to a group of terrorists that had to be kept out, were border controls. Sometimes they were introduced as part of a domino effect caused by one of the countries' other measures. When Belgium closed its restaurants, bars and non-essential shops, Belgians a bit short on public responsibility simply went shopping, dining and partying just across the border in the Netherlands, where these places were still open. The Belgian authorities (not to mention the virologists) were furious: people could become infected in a Dutch bar and bring the virus back to Belgium, making the measures they had introduced worthless. Local Dutch mayors were not very happy either – an explosion of 'bar tourism' in a region that was already heavily affected by COVID-19 would only make things worse. The solution? Belgium reinstalled border controls. As of 20 March, the borders were closed for all non-essential journeys.

By then, several Schengen countries had reintroduced border checks, after some initial reluctance. At the beginning of March Italy had bent over backwards to keep their borders open. But on 11 March – the day after European leaders called for 'a joint European approach' – Slovenia shut down most of its rail and road connections with Italy. So did Austria. It appeared that closing borders had become a global craze that day: on the other side of the Atlantic Ocean US president Donald Trump announced restrictions on travellers coming from Schengen countries. The US border was de facto closed for Europeans.

Over the next few days, the Slovenian and Austrian examples caught on. Poland, which had already introduced temperature checks for bus, van and ferry passengers, reinstalled border checks with Germany. Immediately, hundreds of Baltic truck drivers were stuck at the Polish-German border and the Baltic countries were closed off from their supply routes. When Croatia introduced border restrictions, people were stuck on buses in massive traffic jams for over 48 hours. Some countries still allowed their own citizens or people with their main or second residence there to return, on the condition they spent 14 days at home, in quarantine. The Czech Republic went a step further: people from fifteen countries, including from several EU partners, were banned from entering the country. Czechs themselves were no longer allowed to visit those fifteen countries either. Hungary also took some tough measures: the government imposed border controls with neighbouring Schengen countries Austria and Slovenia, and closed its border for people coming from Italy. In one go, Hungary's Orbán government used the COVID-19 crisis to suspend all asylum seekers' applications, 'as part of the fight against corona'. He was not the only one. 'In a health emergency, this country is not a safe port for migrants', the Maltese prime minister Robert Abela said. And in late February, Greece had also upgraded its border controls to prevent, in the words of prime minister Kyriakos Mitsotakis, 'migrants infected with the Coronavirus from entering the EU'. To 'protect' Greek islands like Lesbos and Chios, the Greek coastguard increased its patrols in the Eastern Aegean.

Most European countries, however, claimed health reasons, not migration, to justify border checks. On 18 March, it was Germany's turn. Europe's biggest economy (partially) 'closed' its borders with five neighbouring countries: Austria, France, Denmark, Luxembourg and Switzerland. Just like other European countries, the borders were not technically closed, the German authorities were quick to emphasise. Closing the border, 'that's what North Korea does', explained federal police chief Dieter Romann. Commuters and goods were still allowed to cross the border. German nationals and resident foreigners could also return home. But for all other border crossings you needed a very good reason. 'As long as there is no European solution', German interior minister Seehofer argued, 'you must act in the interest of your own population'. Let's hope it's only for a short period, chancellor Merkel added.

By 20 March, seventeen out of the 26 Schengen countries had taken their borders into their own hands. Legally, this was allowed. The so-called 2013 Schengen Borders Code, which contains all the rules on how Schengen works, allows countries to carry out controls in the regions around the border or, as a last resort, to reinstall border controls in case of a 'serious threat to public policy or internal security'. On the condition that these controls were proportionate and temporary (they could be extended for up to two years), and that they notified the other Schengen countries and the European institutions. The real problem, however, was that certainly in the beginning there was very little coordination and communication between the countries, to the regret of Commission president von der Leyen. She had to accept that certain controls were put in place but at the same time continued to speak out against general travel bans. 'At the moment that we speak', her spokesperson said a day after the German decision, 'the virus is already present in all European Member States. Therefore, closing borders is not necessarily the best way of ensuring that we contain further the outbreak within the EU'. Not only was it not very effective, it also had a major socio-economic impact and disrupted the daily lives of citizens.

FROM NATIONAL MEASURES TO A EUROPEAN SOLUTION

Seehofer's comment on the need for a European solution was interesting: national measures were necessary 'as long as there is no European solution'. A European solution is also what president Emmanuel Macron had hinted at in his address to the French nation on 12 March, when the first border controls appeared: 'We will, without any doubt, have to take measures, but we have to take them to reduce contact between affected zones and non-affected ones. This is not necessarily about national borders (…) There will, for sure, be border controls or closures, but such measures have to be taken when they are relevant, and we have to take them as Europeans, at the European level.'

A couple of days later the Commission came up with a European solution: in order to keep internal borders open, the virus had to be stopped at Europe's external borders. Everyone entering the Schengen zone had to undergo a health check upon arrival. Non-Europeans not living in Europe who had symptoms, or could have come into contact with infected people, could just be turned away. This was not a travel ban or a border closure as such: non-Europeans could still come to Europe if they had a good reason. Goods could come in. People working in the transport sector, health workers and some other categories of people could get in. But travellers on a non-essential trip were no longer allowed into the EU. Tough luck for anyone wanting a holiday or to visit family living there.

Ursula von der Leyen hoped that the decision to better control Europe's borders would restore trust and lessen the need for internal border checks. If your front door is being closely watched, there's no need to lock the doors of your rooms.

The timing of the Commission's proposal, 15 March, was no coincidence. It was two days before the European leaders had another videoconference, the second since the start of the crisis. During the videoconference, the countries promptly endorsed the Commission's proposal. This was more than just a formality. After all, according to European law, it was only the countries who could implement the Commission's proposal. It is not the Commission that can install controls at the EU's external border; it is not the Commission that can check who gets in and who doesn't. That is down to each individual country. Legally, therefore, it was not a European decision, but a coordinated set of national decisions, as the Commission's spokesperson on migration Adalbert Jahnz put it.

This of course gave quite some flexibility to the nations. In principle, each government could decide for itself what it considered 'an essential trip'. And each could decide whether to quarantine arrivals or not. But since the Commission came up with rather detailed guidance on how to implement the measures, and since this guidance was endorsed by the European Council, the countries had to, 'in the spirit of Schengen cooperation', toe the line. You could be forgiven for thinking at this point that having one European decision for the entire region would be much easier. But so long as the law remains unchanged, this kind of coordinated action is probably the best one could hope for.

Nevertheless, the hope that countries would ease their internal border restrictions didn't bear fruit. In the days after the European Council's second videoconference on 17 March, border restrictions within the Schengen area remained. New ones were even introduced, by Germany and Belgium among others. The result was a pretty chaotic patchwork. Entering Austria was only possible at some border crossings. And unless you could show a recent health certificate you had to spend 14 days in quarantine on arrival. Crossing the Czech-German border was also allowed at certain places only. Cross-border workers travelling from France into Belgium had to show a document from their employer stating that this was a work-related 'essential' trip. A Belgian who wanted to pick up a relative at Charles De Gaulle Airport in Paris also needed to produce proof: a copy of the plane ticket or a document confirming their relationship. And what about a weekend trip from Denmark to Poland? Forget it, unless you were Polish, married to a Pole, had a work permit or a residence card. On 26 March, 25 years after Schengen was born, the founding fathers probably had a very different anniversary in mind.

Somehow the patchwork of different border controls had to be managed. In an attempt to keep things moving within the EU, commissioner Ylva Johansson, in charge of Home Affairs, presented a series of 'guidelines'. Since border control is a national responsibility, the Commission had little power. It could only issue guidance and recommendations. When more and more practical problems popped up, from citizens being stuck in neighbouring countries to seasonal workers being stopped at the border, the Commission created a group where it could, together with the countries, discuss (and solve) all border-related problems: the 'COVID-19/Corona Information Group – Home Affairs'. A group that clearly showed that reinstalling border controls is easier said than done!

The restrictions on free movement of people led to a host of practical problems, with a huge economic impact. A first concern were cross-border and seasonal workers. The same countries that had (partially) closed their own borders still needed their citizens employed in a neighbouring country to be able to get to work. Hungary had restricted access for everyone who did not live there, but 2% of its workforce had a job in Austria or Slovenia. So Hungary had to find an arrangement with those countries so that its citizens were allowed through.

FOCUS ON:

The COVID-19/Corona Information Group

This is a technical forum created on 26 February in which EU countries and the Commission discuss cross-border problems. All issues related to the free movement of people, obstacles at border crossings or the management of the external border are up for discussion. It meets once or twice a week and is chaired by the Directorate-General for Migration and Home Affairs (HOME) of the European Commission. The name 'Information Group' illustrates its limited decision-making powers.

Seasonal workers too required special attention. In the region where I live, fruit and vegetable growers rely on seasonal workers, mainly from Poland, Bulgaria and Romania, to pick strawberries, tomatoes and especially asparagus. In the Netherlands, one third of all fruit and vegetable companies employ seasonal workers. But because of the restrictions at the borders, they were discouraged from travelling. This not only had serious social and economic consequences, it also had a negative impact on food supply. To ensure they could continue their work, the Commission recommended giving them 'special category' status, like health workers, and waving them through.

Another group that fell victim to the uncoordinated border restrictions were the thousands of Europeans who were trapped outside the EU and were trying to get back home. If a Spanish student studying in India got a seat on a German repatriation flight from New Delhi to Frankfurt, they were not yet home. They still had to get from Frankfurt to Spain. They first had to get a green light to enter Germany (even though they were not a German citizen) and then had to be allowed to continue onto Spain. The Commission guidelines therefore explicitly asked countries to make sure that EU citizens who wanted to go home could do so. But what the Commission recommended for seasonal workers, cross-border workers and citizens returning home were just guidelines. Nothing was legally binding. More than once, the Council or even the European Council had to step in to make sure that these guidelines were followed on the ground, at each airport, at every border crossing. This was a process with many ups-and-downs. Take the example of the stranded travellers. Foreign ministers discussed this at their meeting on 23 March. The leaders did the same at their videoconference three days later. 'Where temporary internal border controls have been introduced, we will ensure smooth border management for persons and goods (…) We will urgently address (…) the remaining problems concerning EU citizens blocked at internal EU borders and prevented from returning to their home countries', they solemnly declared. But the Commission once again had to make the point at another foreign ministers' meeting ten days later: 'We urge you to ensure that the principles contained in our guidance, namely that EU citizens should be allowed to transit through Member States on their way home, is clearly communicated to the relevant national authorities. Border guards need to be fully aware that EU citizens must be able to transit swiftly.' All in all, it took about a month before most of all the practical loopholes had been addressed. It would appear that guidelines, too, have their boundaries.

REOPENING THE BORDERS

The way in which border controls had been reintroduced in mid-March was pretty messy. No one would argue with that. So when it came to reopening the borders, this needed to be done in a more coordinated way. Of course, just like installing them, lifting border controls was also a national decision. And each country was in a different phase of the health crisis, so some preferred to lift restrictions sooner than others. But what was agreed on was the importance of keeping each other well-informed and of a 'phased and coordinated process'.

That required a common framework. Commission president von der Leyen, together with European Council president Michel, started working on guidance, recommendations on how to get out of the lockdown. On 15 April, they presented their 'Joint Roadmap towards lifting COVID-19 containment measures'.

On the topic of border controls the Joint Roadmap was

still rather vague. In mid-April this was too soon anyway. But by the end of the month the health situation started to improve throughout Europe. Most countries noted a substantial decrease in COVID-19 cases. In the third week of April most had passed their peak. Gradually they could start thinking about removing the temporary border controls and returning to open borders within Schengen. In early May, the countries' plans to dismantle their border checks started to take shape. One of the first initiatives, on 6 May, was the announcement by the prime ministers of the three Baltic countries (Estonia, Latvia and Lithuania) to lift all travel restrictions within that area from 15 May. Poland and Finland were granted membership to this mini borderless club a bit later on. Meanwhile, Croatia started conversations with the Czech Republic on an 'air corridor' between the two countries, so that Czechs could spend their summer holidays at the Croatian coast. Austria wanted to attract German tourists, and so looked for an arrangement with Germany to get rid of quarantine rules.

To streamline these regional initiatives, on 13 May the Commission presented guidelines with a specific focus on tourism. As a first step, they recommended restoring the free movement of people between regions and countries 'with sufficiently similar epidemiological situations', based on information provided by the European Centre for Disease Prevention and Control. This way, at least some summer holidays could be saved. But this was not just about people getting their annual dose of sun, sea and sand. Tourism represents more than 11% of employment in the EU and almost 10% of the European economy. In the days that followed the Commission's recommendation, several countries announced a return to open borders. Slovenia's borders would be open for all Europeans by 31 May. Italy, where tourism accounts for

13% of its GDP, said that all borders would be open for EU citizens from 3 June. Greece was to be open for business from 1 July. On the same day, Germany dipped its toe in the water and announced that permanent border checks would be gradually dismantled.

Just like when the border checks were brought in, getting rid of them caused quite some confusion in the border regions. From 30 May, for example, Belgians were allowed to shop or meet family in neighbouring countries. But since France decided to keep its border closed for non-essential trips, the Belgian decision did not apply there, a nuance missed by many people who rushed to see family members living in France. Hundreds were turned away at the French border. A week later, Spain announced to the press that it would reopen its borders with Portugal and France later in June. But Portugal, which had not been informed, disagreed, so Spain had to reconsider its decision.

The situation at the internal and external borders remained complicated and confusing until the decision was taken, by late June, to lift all travel restrictions within the Schengen zone. When that was achieved, another discussion could start, on whether (and how) to lift the ban on travel from third countries into the EU. This was by no means an easy one, especially with the number of infections outside Europe increasing every day. Some European countries took a very cautious position and argued in favour of a limited list of reliable countries such as Canada, Australia, New Zealand and South Korea, where the number of new infections was comparable to the Union. For other European countries such a short list would be a nightmare for their tourism sector. Still others tried to get countries on the list with which they had particularly strong bilateral relations, such as Portugal with Angola, Poland with the United States, or France with Morocco, Tunisia and Algeria.

On 30 June, the European Union agreed on a first list of 14 countries, to be reviewed every two weeks. China was added as number 15 on the condition that it would open its own borders for EU-citizens. The United States, where at that moment more than 2.6 million citizens were infected, did not make the cut. The outcome was far from ideal and in any case not legally binding. It was just a recommendation. After all, border control is a national competence, not a European one. But now that the internal borders were open, the EU countries knew all too well that a coordinated approach was not only nice to have, but a pressing necessity. The alternative would be a chaotic and messy holiday season.

RETURN TO SCHENGEN

During the peak of the COVID-19 crisis, just like in 2015 and 2016, the death knell of Schengen was already being rung. 'Coronavirus Nightmare Could Be the End for Europe's Borderless Dream', *The New York Times* wrote on 26 February. Others spoke of Schengen's near-death experience. Post-corona, Schengen would never be completely borderless.

Every crisis has its lingering cough. More than four years after the peak of the migration crisis, several countries were still checking passports. But might it be possible that Schengen comes out of this crisis stronger? Over the years we have gotten so used to this border-free area that we started to take it for granted. The crisis changed that. Many people rediscovered the importance of Schengen, for their job, meeting family and friends, even just for the weekly shop. Cross-border freedom of movement is a fundamental part of our European way of life. European commissioner for home affairs Ylva Johansson summarised this sentiment as follows: 'It could be a lesson learned that member states would like to see a stronger coordination and more of the Commission in areas where the Commission traditionally does not have the competence.' One area she clearly had in mind was border management in an emergency situation.

To keep it that way, two things matter in the short-term. Firstly, it cannot be said enough that internal border controls ('taking back control') do not address the real problem we want to solve. The fight against terrorism, cross-border organised crime or illegal migration will not be won by closing the borders, simply because they are not caused by a lack of borders in the Schengen Area. Tackling terrorism requires first and foremost a better exchange of intelligence, while the fight against illegal migration needs a foreign and development policy that address the reasons why people leave their countries in the first place. The same applies to fighting a pandemic. Health experts have said repeatedly that border restrictions could temporarily slow down the spread of the virus, but that testing and contact tracing are far more effective. And they don't come with negative side effects either, like disruption to the supply of food and medicines.

Secondly, strengthening the external borders of Schengen remains crucial and urgent to restore credibility and trust. When it comes to overhauling the European asylum and migration system, European leaders have to bite the bullet. But as this crisis has shown, solid external borders are also important from a health perspective. COVID-19 will not be the last pandemic. The better prepared the EU is to efficiently manage its external borders, the less it will have to improvise when the time comes.

CHAPTER 11

Money, Money, Money

How finance ministers found €540 billion to keep the economy going
- Why no-one worried too much about rising public debt
- What the different European banks did to try and save jobs

Managing Schengen was not easy. But the fourth priority put forward by European leaders on 10 March was probably even more complex: to tackle the socio-economic consequences of the COVID-19 crisis. The 2007-2008 financial and economic crisis started in the economy's nervous system, the banking sector. In 2020, the reason for the economic downturn lay outside the economic system, in the measures governments took to curtail the spread of the virus.

The COVID-19 virus shook both supply and demand: it affected the supply of goods and services as well as the demand for them. Lockdown and physical distancing measures forced companies and shops to close down, especially when the (for most of Europe) 1.5 metre distance could not be guaranteed. The more people ended up in quarantine or had to stay home, the less goods or services they could produce professionally. People were no longer allowed to travel, go to the cinema or to the shoe shop around the corner, so demand for these products dropped, sometimes dramatically. According to the think tank Copenhagen Economics, economic activity decreased by more than a quarter overall. Some sectors were less hit than others. In the technology sector, for instance, activity was reduced by 'only' 15%. But in the cultural and entertainment sector, in restaurants and hotels and in part of the retail sector, the situation was far from rosy. These sectors had to survive on just 15 to 25% of their normal activity. The European tourism industry, for example, lost €1 billion a month!

The socio-economic consequences of the emergency response were brutal. Decision-makers had to put the economy into a temporary coma. This was not always a popular decision but it was necessary to prevent more serious damage. If there were a second virus peak, new lockdown measures could lead to a 16% drop in the European GDP. Then we would really be in trouble. Unlike US president Trump and Brazilian president Bolsonaro, European leaders walked a tightrope between health and wealth. When on 16 March the French president Macron addressed the nation on television he called on the French government and parliament to only focus on fighting the epidemic. All energy, all power had to be channelled into achieving one single goal: slowing down the virus. But a bit later in his speech he also declared that no French company should risk bankruptcy. 'Count on us to save our economy and to give certainty to all workers'.

That same evening, I watched Dutch prime minister Mark Rutte's TV address. 'We cannot close our eyes for the economic consequences of the virus', he said, in that typically Dutch level-headed and down-to-earth tone. The lady that runs the coffeeshop on the corner, the florist, the transport provider, the national airline KLM… the government promised to do all it could to support them and make sure that people did not lose their jobs. In most of the speeches by European leaders it was easy to spot what the American business magazine *Forbes* described as a balancing act between three objectives. First, the need to effectively combat the virus. Second, to provide substantial financial support to the millions of furloughed workers as well as small and large businesses. Third, to kickstart the economy. Health, wealth, jobs. Three corners of the same triangle. High healthcare costs are an economic killer; no strong healthcare system can be built on an economic wasteland; and no economy thrives without healthy workers and employees. The economy was on life support but the vital organs should continue to function. When the economy wakes up, it would need companies, big and small, and jobs. Liquidity and job support were the two buzzwords at this stage of the economic crisis. Both were also explicitly mentioned by the European leaders in their wrap-up of the 10 March videoconference.

LIQUIDITY

The liquidity of a company indicates whether it can pay its short-term bills or not. If it can't, because it doesn't have enough money in its bank account, it risks bankruptcy. During the COVID-19 crisis companies saw their revenue plummet, but they still had bills to pay. Liquidity became a real challenge. Some entrepreneurs got very creative. When a friend of mine, an optician, had to close his shop, he quickly set up a 'glasses delivery service'. And the restaurant next door transformed itself into a 'take away' snackbar. This brought some relief for the owners, but not enough: all eyes were on the government. Each country came up with its own package of support measures. Several countries provided extra state guarantees to banks so that they were more inclined to quickly provide liquidity to any (healthy) company that needed it. In France, the government decided to suspend electricity, water and gas bills for smaller companies. In Belgium, small and medium businesses received a one-time financial compensation for the days they were closed. In Denmark, event management companies that saw their events cancelled because of COVID-19 could count on government support. Germany reserved €100 billion to buy stocks in companies that were severely affected by the coronacrisis. Many countries allowed firms to delay paying their taxes or social contributions until they were back in business and had fresh income. These and other similar measures all served the same purpose: to make sure that companies that were in good shape before the crisis would be back up and running when the economy awoke from its coma.

JOBS

A second priority was to ensure that people did not lose their jobs. If a company (temporarily) has no economic activity and no revenue, it might have to lay off part of its workforce, only to then recruit them (or others) later on. This is in no-one's interest. To avoid such lay-offs most countries established or extended what is known as a short-time work scheme. This meant a company could temporarily reduce working hours (even to zero), and the government would pay the employees the rest. Similar arrangements were put in place for self-employed workers, to make sure that they too would stay afloat. All over Europe, millions of workers adopted new short-time systems. In Germany, around 6% were in 'Kurzarbeit'. In Belgium, at the peak of the pandemic, 1.3 million workers made use of this system. This kind of scheme wasn't completely new to some countries, but the numbers certainly were.

The measures to preserve liquidity and jobs didn't come cheap for national governments. On top of that, they had to increase medical spending. They needed additional money to buy face masks and other medical supplies or to increase the capacity of hospitals and retirement homes. Several of them also increased social support. Spain, for instance, issued meal allowances to ensure that vulnerable children had basic access to food.

All together, we are talking billions and billions of euros in additional public spending and lost public revenue. This had a huge (negative) impact on national budgets. In May 2020, the European Commission expected that France, Spain and Italy would face budget deficits of 10% or more. Even Germany, which last year still had a budget surplus of 1.5%, would move to a deficit of 5.5%. Seven of the 19 eurozone countries were expected to have 2020 debt levels of more than 100%.

Such levels of government spending were only possible if the European framework were changed on at least two fronts. Both the Stability and Growth Pact (SGP) and the state aid rules had be adjusted. What would have been unthinkable in normal circumstances, now happened with hardly any discussion at all: both frameworks were temporarily put on ice.

This was especially remarkable for the Stability and Growth Pact. Since it entered into force in 1999, the SGP has been at the centre of many political, even ideological, discussions. In essence, it is a set of rules that ensures that countries, especially those that use the euro, do not spend more money than is considered good for them. First-ly, a government has to make sure that its budget does not have a deficit that exceeds 3% of its GDP. In other words, a country cannot spend more than 3% of what it receives through taxes and other revenue. In 2019, Spain and France were very close to that threshold. Secondly, a country's total public debt could not be higher than 60% of its GDP. In 2019, Greece, Italy and Portugal were above 100%, and Belgium was skating on thin ice. If a country's total debt does go above 60% of its GDP, it has to show that it is making serious efforts to bring it down. If it repeatedly breaks these rules, it could be fined.

Some countries, mainly from northern Europe, argue that respect for these rules is essential for the stability of the eurozone. A common currency can only work if all countries that are part of it keep their public finances healthy. For others, mostly from the southern part of Europe, these rules are way too strict. Because of this straitjacket, governments cannot properly invest in areas that promote growth, such as research or economic infrastructure. In an op-ed in *The Financial Times* in October 2014, former Italian prime minister Mario Monti summed it up very well: 'Europe can no longer afford to stick with such a rudimentary instrument. By failing to recognize the proper role of public investment, it has pushed governments to stop building infrastructure just when they should have built more.'

FOCUS ON:

The Stability and Growth Pact

The Stability and Growth Pact was agreed on by the EU countries in 1997. The idea was to better monitor how each country deals with its budget. This was a logical extension to the fact that countries shared a common currency. Under the SGP, each year the European Commission analyses the national budgets and comes up with recommendations. If a country breaches the rules it has to take corrective action. The SGP dates back to a 1995 proposal by the German finance minister Theo Waigel. Around the same time he also launched the name 'euro' for the common currency.

The tension between those in favour of strict budgetary controls (in other words, 'austerity') and those preferring more public spending can be felt at any discussion on the Stability and Growth Pact. The first group calls for the strict implementation of the (binding) Pact. They generally have their budget in order. The second group wants (and needs) more flexibility. When Ursula von der Leyen first addressed the European Parliament, as candidate for Commission president, she tried to find a middle ground: 'We need to work within the Stability and Growth Pact. Where investment and reforms are needed we should make sure they can be done. We should make use of all the flexibility allowed in the rules.'

That was in July 2019. COVID-19 put this discussion on hold. Instead of allowing some flexibility in some areas (for instance more government spending on health), the finance ministers decided on 23 March to simply suspend all obligations under the Stability and Growth Pact. By activating the so-called 'general escape clause', for the first time ever, countries could spend as much as they needed. The countries got 'carte blanche' to fight the crisis, to make sure their economies remained afloat and their healthcare system continued to function. This was a drastic decision, but by all means a wise one. After all, it would be hard to imagine that in the midst of the worst crisis since World War II, countries and the Commission would want to spend their time quibbling over the rule-book. But maybe more to the point, too many countries had already 'broken the rules' anyway.

A second set of rules that mattered in this context were the state aid rules. While the Stability and Growth Pact mainly defines how much money governments can spend, the European state aid rules give guidance on what to spend it on. Or rather, on what not. Under normal circumstances, the Commission is a rather tough 'state aid watchdog'. And rightly so. If a government helps one of its companies, for instance by giving subsidies, cheap loans or a lower tax regime, then that company gets an advantage over competing companies in a country that does not have the same deep pockets. Not every country can deploy a €1.2 trillion rescue package, like Germany did in this crisis. Or even worse, in a single market with no borders, a company could simply close its offices and move to a country where it got more financial support. To avoid that kind of internal competition within the EU, the Commission wants to make sure that companies are treated equally, regardless of where they are located.

During the exceptional circumstances brought about by the coronacrisis, these state aid rules got about as bendy as the SGP rules. If a government wanted to help a national company to 'repurpose' their production lines and produce much-needed medical products, or if it wanted to provide cheap loans or tax breaks to give companies more liquidity, then they just told the Commission, who in turn gave them the green light without too much discussion. 'A la guerre comme à la guerre', as the French say.

Even though such measures were necessary at that very moment, they came with significant side effects. Countries that could afford it – I gave the example of Germany which took measures equivalent to more than 40% of its GDP – took unprecedented measures to support their economies. Others with less budgetary capacity, such as Italy, Spain or even France, couldn't afford to do that. Over time, this could lead to increasing economic, financial and also social divergences within the Eurozone. If not addressed, these differences could even threaten the stability of the euro. As soon as the worst of the COVID crisis was over, this issue had to be tackled.

MORE MONEY, FROM EUROPE

Faced with an economic shock that was much more severe – but radically different – than the one in 2007-2008, national governments needed maximum flexibility to provide assistance. The flexibility under the state aid rules and the Stability and Growth Pact allowed countries to spend money from their national budgets. But they were not alone to carry the burden of higher spending. On top of national money, European money could be mobilised. Discussions on how to do this dominated most of the months of March and April 2020. Finding European money to fund the most pressing needs was a battle fought on many fronts. The key players in this fight were the European Central Bank, the European Commission and the Eurogroup.

Let's start with the European Central Bank (ECB). As soon as the economic crisis became clear, all eyes were on Frankfurt, where the bank has its headquarters. On the economic chess board, the ECB is the queen of monetary policy. She controls how much money flows into the economy. When your high-street banks – BNP Paribas, Banco Santander, Rabobank etc – borrow money from the ECB, they pay interest. If the ECB decides to lower its interest rates on such loans (what it has been doing for quite some time now), it becomes cheaper for banks to borrow. As a result, it also becomes cheaper for companies and people like us to borrow money from our bank for things like upgrading our equipment or finally buying that dream home. Money 'becomes cheaper', and more of it enters into the real economy. That's the idea.

Another way to achieve the same result is by manipulating the so-called deposit interest rate. Commercial banks have the habit of giving their excess cash to the ECB for safe keeping. But the ECB can use interest rates to charge them for this service which allows them to essentially tell the banks: don't put your cash here, lend it to businesses and consumers instead. The result is, once again: more money that flows into the real economy.

Manipulating its interest rates was one way for the ECB to inject cheaper money into the economy. But that was not the only trick the bank had up its sleeve. Five years ago, to address the fallout of the eurocrisis, the ECB added something more controversial to its toolbox: 'quantitative easing' ('QE'). A first, cautious step was taken on 10 May 2010, after a weekend in which Europe's leaders worked day and night to save the euro. Well-hidden in a pretty incomprehensible press release, the ECB announced that it would buy, under very strict conditions, a limited number of government bonds, debt issued by eurozone governments, from private investors such as banks. As a result, more money entered the banks, interest rates got lower, money became cheaper, companies and consumers could borrow more and had to spend less to repay their loans, all of which leads to more spending and more investment, more economic growth and more jobs. Two years later, in August 2012, ECB president Draghi again made use of such a tool, to deliver on his renowned promise to do 'whatever it takes to save the euro'. By 2014, the ECB had gotten quite used to this and extended the scope of the programme: 'quantitative easing' was born. Developed in a gradual way, it undoubtedly played an important role in bringing the eurocrisis under control.

This time, when the COVID-19 crisis began to infect the European economy, the ECB was much more cautious at first. It announced that it would buy government bonds for another €120 billion. But at the same time, in its press conference on 12 March, the new ECB president Lagarde was pretty blunt. Freely translated, her message to EU countries was: Don't put, once again, the onus for fixing the crisis on the ECB. There will be no 'Whatever It Takes No.2'. In other words, governments had to use their own money, their own budget, to help their companies or to support workers in short-time work and not only rely on money they get from selling their debt to the ECB.

It is now largely forgotten, but this reaction was not all that different from the initial reaction to the banking crisis in 2010. Back then, countries with high levels of debt like France, Italy, Spain and Portugal also asked the (politically independent) ECB to buy government debt. But the ECB (and German chancellor Merkel) refused. It was only after European leaders had clearly committed themselves to 'take all measures needed' to get their public finances under control, that the ECB publicly stated that it would step in. The ECB would get most of the credit for 'saving the euro', but it was the European leaders that got the ball rolling. In other words, first countries had to show their cards, only then would the ECB take action. That's also what was at play in March 2020. Lagarde was looking to the countries to make the first move. But the reactions to Lagarde's press conference were devastating: the measures she announced were not enough. Italian president Sergio Mattarella was hurt; he expected 'solidarity rather than obstacles'. The market did not appreciate Lagarde's comments either, the Milan stock exchange lost 17% that day. Less than a week later, on 18 March, the ECB corrected its position and launched a new 'QE' programme: the 'Pandemic Emergency Purchase Programme' (PEPP). Under this programme, the bank would buy, without too many restrictions, government and corporate bonds for a total value of €750 billion. 'Extraordinary times require extraordinary action', Lagarde said when she presented the measure. Interestingly enough, the ECB decided to buy bonds of governments that needed the money most. In the past, it bought bonds according to how much each country contributed to the capital of the bank. By buying more from countries like Italy and Spain, an element of solidarity snuck into the ECB's policies. Later on, in May, it added another €600 billion to PEPP. So, €1350 billion, on top of the initial €120 billion of national debt was sold to the ECB during the peak of the COVID-19 crisis. An enormous amount, but still only half of what the American central bank bought in the US. Bottom line: the tools that during the previous crisis still had to be invented from scratch, were now available and, after some initial hesitation, effectively used. With that, the ECB had done its part of the job.

By then, our second player the European Commission, the king on the economic chessboard, had gone through all its programmes with a fine-toothed comb. They started looking for unspent money from the 2020 budget. The idea was to redirect every unused euro to fight the COVID-19 crisis. Part of the untouched funds – some €2.7 billion – was channelled into the Emergency Support Instrument (ESI). The ESI was originally created in 2016 to give emergency assistance to countries that were heavily affected by the huge influx of refugees and migrants. But back then, it was decided that the ESI could also be used to address other serious humanitarian crises, such as terrorist attacks and epidemics. On 2 April, it was re-activated to support emergency healthcare in the EU. It could be used to buy medical infrastructure or to support companies that changed their production lines to produce medical equipment. Or if a country felt enough solidarity to treat a patient of another country, then it could use ESI funding to transport them.

Quite some spare cash was also found in the so-called cohesion funds, the money used to close the financial gap between regions and countries in the EU. Some years ago, when travelling through Bulgaria, I visited the region around Veliko Tarnovo. That city had been an important cultural centre in the middle ages and is still extremely picturesque (it was a great holiday!). But at the same time, it was hard to believe that this region belonged to the same union as – say – the region around Hamburg. Europe's diversity is shown in the figures: the GDP per capita of Luxembourg is 12 times that of Bulgaria; the Luxembourg government spends 17 times more money on healthcare than its Bulgarian counterpart; the average wages are eight times greater in the small duchy and life expectancy there is seven years higher than in Bulgaria. That is what cohesion money is for.

To close these gaps, a handful of cohesion funds were created over the years. In the period 2014-2020, this cohesion money amounted to more than €350 billion. With the money that had not been used in 2019, the Commission created a 'Corona' fund, the 'Corona Response Investment Initiative Plus' (CRII). Countries could spend this money (initially some €8 billion) on pretty much whatever they liked, without necessarily following all the strict rules that normally come with these cohesion funds. They could use it to support their small and medium business, to buy ventilators or kits, or to pay for short-time work schemes. The same flexibility would now also apply to the EU Solidarity Fund. The initial goal of that fund was to help countries affected by natural disasters. But now countries could use the funding of up to €800 million to fight the new coronavirus.

While the European Central Bank was pumping more money into the blood vessels of Europe's economic tissue and the European Commission was mobilising all the unused money to support countries, a third key player, the 19 finance ministers of the Eurogroup had not been resting on their laurels. Together with the Commission, they had started to work on a multi-billion dollar rescue package, as the European Council had asked on 10 March. From the beginning, they also involved their eight non-euro colleagues in the discussions. On 9 April, a month after the request of the European Council, the finance ministers reached an agreement on a €540 billion package.

The discussions on this package had their fair share of drama. The discussions went back and forth between the 27 finance ministers and the European Council. After each meeting of ministers, the Eurogroup reported back to the European Council, where the prime ministers, presidents or chancellors took a closer look at the progress made and encouraged them to continue their work. Eight meetings in total. Or more precisely: eight videoconferences.

The €540 billion package that the finance ministers finally agreed on was meant to supplement the money that national governments were spending. The package consists of three different parts: one to help workers, one to support companies, and one to feed the budgets of the national governments.

The support for workers got the short and sweet name SURE (its full name was typical EU jargon: 'Support to mitigate Unemployment Risks in an Emergency'). Under SURE, a government that needed money to finance its national short-time work schemes or to support self-employed workers who temporarily lost income could borrow money from the EU. For most countries, borrowing from the EU was cheaper than borrowing directly from the market. The EU has a very good financial reputation, a so-called triple A rating, which only a few euro members have: Germany, Luxembourg and the Netherlands. With the EU budget and national contributions as a guarantee, the EU would borrow €100 billion on the market at very low interest rates, and then give loans, at the same low interest rates and with very few conditions, to the countries that asked for one. 'Solidarity at work', von der Leyen called it. A clear advantage of being part of a bigger club.

Some type of European unemployment reinsurance scheme that could protect citizens during serious economic shocks was already foreseen when the Commission took office, in late 2019. The COVID-19 crisis accelerated the work. In the discussions that took place in March 2020, an interesting divergence of ideas popped up between northern and southern European countries, as is often the case with socio-economic issues. The main antagonists were Spain and the Netherlands. For the Netherlands, SURE was strictly linked to the COVID-19 crisis and a temporary thing, just like the short-time work schemes. It could only be used 'for the duration of the emergency' and for 'the specific emergency circumstances of the COVID-19 crisis'.

Spain however looked a bit further ahead. As a result of the COVID-19 crisis, millions of Europeans would end up in unemployment. According to a rather pessimistic McKinsey scenario, 59 million jobs in Europe were at risk. Many temporary contracts would not be renewed, many self-employed would not re-open their shop or restaurant. This meant, Spain argued, that countries will face higher costs for unemployment benefits for a considerable time to come. Shouldn't SURE then become a more permanent fixture, to help countries cover the costs of their unemployment schemes as well? That's why Spain wanted SURE to develop into a fund that could assist countries confronted with a sudden rise in unemployment. But the 'SUREly-not' camp, led by the Netherlands, insisted that the final agreement of 9 April stated that SURE did 'not pre-judge the position on future proposals related to unemployment insurance'. Post-COVID-19, the discussion will no doubt return.

The part of the €540 billion package for companies – good for €200 billion – was less contentious. This was mainly in the hands of that other European Bank: the European Investment Bank (EIB). Unlike the European Central Bank (the bank of the 19 eurozone countries), the European Investment Bank (the bank of all 27 EU countries) does not deal with preserving price stability or setting interest rates. The EIB is literally the bank of the EU. Both were created in 1958 and share a common history. The EIB borrows money on the capital market on very favourable terms (because no one doubts that the EIB will diligently pay it back). The bank then invests the money in projects that are closely linked to the objectives of the European Union.

In response to the COVID-19 pandemic, in early March the EIB had adopted an emergency plan that would mobilise up to €40 billion to support small and medium businesses. In addition to that, and as a contribution to the rescue package of the Eurogroup, the EIB created another fund, the Pan-European Guarantee Fund, specifically dedicated to supporting businesses. This new fund of €25 billion of guarantees enabled local banks or national promotional banks to provide an estimated €200 billion of loans to mainly small and medium enterprises. The ministers welcomed it with open arms. €100 billion from SURE, €200 billion from this Guarantee Fund... the package was taking shape. The last part was the most difficult one. At the core of the discussion was the so-called European Stability Mechanism (ESM). The ESM was created in October 2012, at the end of the eurocrisis. The public debt of several European countries – first Greece, then Spain, Portugal, Italy, Cyprus, Ireland and even France – was reaching such high levels that the markets were afraid that they would no longer be able to pay back their loans. It was increasingly difficult for them to find investors willing to lend them money. And if they did, interest rates were exuberantly high. To help them through this, the finance ministers of the eurozone created a special fund: the ESM. All eurozone members contributed to it, some €80 billion in total, which the ESM could use as a guarantee to raise money under very favourable conditions. With that money, it offered credit lines (loans) to members of the eurozone who were struggling. Once again, it illustrates the enormous advantage of being part of a larger (creditworthy) market player.

The fact that there was something like the ESM now helped the negotiations. In the 2010-2012 crisis, the situation was different. The finance ministers and the European leaders were firefighters without firehoses. They had to manage a totally unpredictable crisis empty handed. There was no recipe, no framework, no handbook to fall back on. Now that the ESM was there, the finance ministers could build on this to create a tool they labelled 'Pandemic Crisis Support'. All eurozone countries could draw from this credit line, up to a maximum of 2% of their 2019 GDP. The costs of borrowing this money were minimal. If all 19 countries maxed out their allowance, the entire thing would amount to no €240 billion.

The main question, however, was: under which conditions could a country get access to this money? During and after the eurocrisis, the rules for using the ESM were rather tough. The country in question had to commit itself to tough economic reforms. It had to take far-reaching measures to make sure that its public debt went down. It had to go through an in-depth analysis and was closely monitored by the so-called troika, composed of the European Commission, the European Central Bank and the IMF. This watchdog role did not make these institutions very popular. When on a weekend trip to Lisbon I told my Airbnb host that I lived in Brussels, she gave me an hour-long lecture about the Brussels Troika. I decided it was best to keep quiet about the fact I worked for the European Commission. In some parts of Europe, conditionality was a sensitive, emotional issue.

How sensitive the issue still was, was probably underestimated by those finance ministers who were now asking again for strict conditions. In late March and early April, this led to bitter fights between the Dutch finance minister Wopke Hoekstra and some southern European countries. When Hoekstra asked Brussels to look into which countries had actually built up a financial buffer, the Portuguese prime minister called the Dutch position 'repugnant'. It reminded him of the Dutch standpoint during the eurocrisis: 'This recurrent pettiness completely undermines what the spirit of the EU is about', he said. On Twitter, the Spanish foreign minister Gonzales was equally scathing: 'Wopke Hoekstra, we are in this EU boat together. We hit an unexpected iceberg. We all share the same risk now. No time for discussions about alleged first and second class tickets'. European Parliament president David Sassoli, an Italian himself, could not resist a subtle reference to the most famous Dutch export product: 'In this moment, we have to strengthen our Union and its market. Countries that are still hesitant about this – who will you sell your technology or tulips to, if the European market is not protected?'

But this was not 2008, 2010 or 2012. Back then, it could be said that the governments that were most in trouble had brought it on themselves. Some had not taken the difficult reforms that others had. Greece had even fudged the numbers it had sent to Brussels. I remember vividly how in 2010 the Slovak prime minister – and later the Slovak parliament – refused to financially contribute to a rescue package for Greece, because the average monthly pension of a Greek worker was three times higher than that of a Slovak worker. Everyone had to take their responsibility, every country had to keep its budget under control, that was the condition.

This time, however, it was a different ball game. No European government was responsible for the COVID-19 outbreak. It would be harsh to blame one or more governments for doing all they could – also financially – to save the lives of their citizens. When that penny dropped, the ministers found a compromise, on 9 April. The conditions for borrowing money were, in the words of the

French finance minister Bruno Le Maire, 'very light'. There was no macro-economic conditionality and no troika process. To appease the northern European countries, it was agreed that the loans could only be used to cover the direct and indirect healthcare costs caused by the COVID-19 crisis, and only until the end of the crisis. 'Afterwards', the agreement said, 'euro area Member States would remain committed to strengthen economic and financial fundamentals, consistent with the EU economic and fiscal coordination and surveillance frameworks'. In other words, as soon as this crisis is over, the conditions would be back.

All in all, this compromise was rather close to what the German (social democratic) ministers of foreign affairs and finance Heiko Maas and Olaf Scholz had suggested in their op-ed published three days earlier in five carefully selected newspapers: *Les Echos* (France), *La Stampa* (Italy), *El País* (Spain), *Público* (Portugal) and *Ta Nea* (Greece). In their article they wrote explicitly that 'The funds must not come with any unnecessary conditions attached, as that would be tantamount to a rerun of the austerity policy that followed the financial crisis (...) We don't need a troika, inspectors, and a reform programme for each country drawn up by the Commission.'

The €240 billion of the ESM credit line made the €540 billion emergence package complete. A relieved president of the Eurogroup quickly sent a letter to European Council president Charles Michel in which he explained the deal. On 23 April, the European Council formally endorsed it, and by 1 June, after some technical finetuning, the measures had entered into force. But this does not mean that suddenly the European 'bank statement' jumped by €540 billion: part of it was money that *could* be mobilised; credit lines that *could* be used. Much depended though on whether countries would actually ask for it or and whether private investors would jump on companies supported by an EIB guarantee. Above all, it was an emergency package, it was short-term life support. But it was a very good first step to save unity, to save the Union.

PART 3

EUROPE REINVENTED

The outbreak of the COVID-19 pandemic caused a systemic shock in Europe. It unsteadied the normal functioning of the European Union. When a country asked for help, solidarity was lacking. Borders between countries, considered a thing of the past, were back. Large parts of the European economy went into lockdown.

As soon as the real impact of the outbreak became clear, the European Union went into emergency mode. Between March and May all energy was pumped into four short-term objectives. Solidarity had to be restored. The single market had to be preserved. The Schengen Area had to be properly managed and re-established as soon as possible. And the European economy had to be put on life support.

By May, much progress had been made in each of these areas. But the pandemic also uncovered some more fundamental, medium to long-term threats. First, when global cooperation was needed more than ever to fight the pandemic, multilateralism groaned under increasing US-Chinese rivalry. Second, the virus highlighted how dependent the EU really was on other powerful global players. Third, worldwide, as in the European Union, fundamental rights and sometimes even the democratic functioning of society were under threat. And finally, the outbreak wreaked economic havoc across Europe's economy, threatening the continent's future economic growth.

Four threats, but also four opportunities for the European Union to emerge from this crisis stronger. Four opportunities for the EU to reinvent itself.

CHAPTER 12

The EU in a G-Zero World Order

- Why COVID-19 will not lead to a radically new world order
- How the EU deals with the US-Chinese rivalry
- Why China sent billions of face masks around the globe

Is COVID-19 calling time on the world order we have known since 1945? A world order that is based on international cooperation, common rules and open trade, with at its core a wide range of international organisations such as the United Nations? Many analysts seem to think so. In their view, the post-World War II order is dead and buried; world leaders have to now sit together and find a new one. Just like they did 75 years ago in Bretton Woods and San Francisco when the world agreed on a common set of rules and principles for the new world order. A world order based on the United Nations, the International Monetary Fund and the World Bank. A new 'San Francisco'-moment or 'Bretton Woods'-moment is needed, analysts say.

Others, such as Harvard professor in international politics Joseph S. Nye Jr., whose books I couldn't get my head out of during my studies, are of a different opinion. Of course, there will be changes, but the pandemic will most likely not prove to be a geopolitical turning point: the balance of power in the world will not change, and COVID-19 will not usher in the end of globalisation.

And then there are those in the middle: change will be fundamental but will not necessarily turn the global order completely upside-down. That is the opinion of French diplomat Michel Duclos who in his blog for the Montaigne Institute called the pandemic a 'geopolitical gamechanger'. Or the French sociologist Dominique Moïsi, author of the 2009 must-read The Geopolitics of Emotion, who also suggested that we are going through a game-changing moment that not only confirms Asia's rise but also reassures that this doesn't mean the decline of the West.

Terms such as 'new world order', 'historical', 'game-changer' or 'epoch-making' should be used sparingly. Internationally speaking, change is gradual. It takes place when a collection of seemingly unrelated events – after some time – form a trend. Some of these events are catalysts. They speed up the trend and can sometimes lead to that one event that formally marks the end of an era. Take the decline of the British Empire. The Maori rebellion against the British in New Zealand in 1860, the Jamaica uprising five years later, the Isandlwana massacre and the Zulu War in 1879, or the British defeats in the 1890 Boer War: all a long time ago now, but each one was a small crack in British global supremacy. The independence of India and Pakistan in 1947 were bigger cracks. But it was the 1956 Suez War that finally smashed the global power of the UK. Another example is the collapse of the USSR. The event that broke it apart is the 1989 fall of the Berlin Wall, but it ended a longer period of decline that had been accelerated by other events, from the Soviet invasion of Afghanistan in 1979 to the Chernobyl disaster in 1986.

Will the COVID-19 outbreak be the smash-event that marks the end of an era, comparable to Britain's 1956-moment or the USSR's 1989-moment, but on a global scale? I am not convinced. But it is definitely one of the cracks, perhaps even a large one. An important accelerator. Like the 9/11 terrorist attacks and the 2008 financial crisis, it speeds up some trends that are crucial for the EU's global position. Let's take a closer look at three of them: the decline of US global leadership, China's rise in soft power and the crisis of multilateral cooperation.

THE DECLINE OF US GLOBAL LEADERSHIP

More than anything else, the COVID-19 outbreak confirms the gradual decline of US global leadership. To a large extent this was a deliberate choice. In his speech to the UN General Assembly in September 2018, president Trump was remarkably blunt: 'America will always choose independence and cooperation over global governance, control, and domination. I honor the right of every nation in this room to pursue its own customs, beliefs, and traditions. The United States will not tell you how to live or work or worship. We only ask that you honor our sovereignty in return.'

In his speech, the president referred ten times to 'sovereignty', to the need to protect and defend the sovereignty of the United States against a global bureaucracy. National interest, summarised by Trump's MAGA (Make America Great Again) beats international engagement. Patriotism trumps multilateralism. International cooperation is 'transactional', a constant search for the best possible deal. Multilateralism and upholding a rules-based international system were not goals but pawns. Perhaps the same could be said of the transatlantic relationship between the US and Europe. After all, the Cold War that glued the US and Europe together is long gone. The logical consequence of all this was that the US started to withdraw from a host of international agreements. They pulled out of the INF Treaty with Russia, an international treaty to eliminate several types of nuclear and conventional missiles. They withdrew from the United Nations Human Rights Council, the historic Paris Climate Agreement, UNESCO, Afghanistan and the UN Global Compact for Migration. Most recently, on 21 May, they withdrew from the Open Skies Treaty, another important part of the international system of arms control. And eight days later, president Trump formally confirmed that the US will terminate their relationship with the World Health Organization, after an initial temporary suspension on funding. Not that it came totally out of the blue. Before the outbreak of the pandemic, the US already planned to cut its contribution by $65 million in 2021. But in the midst of a global health crisis in which *more* international help was needed, not less, this was a strong and unhelpful message.

This trend is not completely new. I remember how in 2011 American diplomats had to explain to their European colleagues that Libya was in Europe's backyard, not the US. It was therefore up to the EU to make sure that the situation there was under control. But the Trump Administration's reluctance to engage internationally went further than any US Administration since World War II. This had implications for America's European partners. After the Trump Administration had blown up the Iranian nuclear deal in the spring of 2018, against the will of the EU, it threatened to cut off all companies, including European ones, from the US market if they still traded with Iran. In other words, the US did not hesitate to use its dominant economic and trade position to pursue its own geopolitical interests. Even at the expense of the security of its European partners. In early 2019, the US threatened a similar move, to sanction German companies that were involved in the construction of the Russian gas pipeline Nord Stream 2.

During the COVID-19 crisis the US continued in the same vein. On 11 March, the president announced on national television that the United States were closing their borders to Europeans as of the next day, without properly warning European leaders. Adding insult to injury, the US blamed this on the 'inaction of EU authorities'. The American attempt to buy a German-based pharmaceutical company in order to get exclusive access to a future vaccine did not go unnoticed either.

COVID-19 confirmed and probably accelerated what Ian Bremmer had predicted in December 2016 in *Time*: 'The Era of American Global Leadership is over'. We have entered a G-zero world, as he called it. And COVID-19 was the first G-zero crisis, in a world with no leadership, with no system manager. This does not mean that the dominant position of the US in economic, military or even cultural terms will soon be overtaken. Far from it. The US will remain the sole superpower for the considerable future. In military terms, it will be a while still before the US has real competition. So it is not so much its hard power position that is at stake now, rather its global leadership position in the multilateral framework. As *The New York Times* pointed out: COVID-19 was the first crisis in more than a century where no one was looking to, or even glancing at, the US for leadership.

CHINA PUMPS SOFT POWER

Unlike the US, China made ample use of the COVID-19 crisis to accelerate its public diplomacy efforts. China beefing up its global image is not new though. Since the early 2000s public diplomacy and what is called 'soft power' policies have become an important part of China's foreign policy. In his 2007 speech to the seventeenth congress of the Chinese Communist Party, then president Hu

Jintao mentioned the deployment of soft power explicitly as an important objective. The state-run media press agency Xinhua and the China Global Television Network were revamped into professional, modern-looking global media outlets, serving a broad global audience.

A core element in Chinese public diplomacy is the superiority of the Chinese model. Strong, centralised state leadership makes it possible to set clear goals, plan well ahead and get things done. A well-organised and disciplined society with a strong sense of civic responsibility take care of the rest. The fact that citizens trust and are loyal to the state guarantees that the plans are effectively implemented. All these elements have contributed to China's stellar growth over the past decades. Neo-Confucian state capitalism pays off, the narrative goes. And it managed to lift 800 million Chinese people out of poverty, setting the bar for other countries with high levels of poverty and underdevelopment.

In COVID-19 times, the same model, with some add-ons like intrusive digital surveillance, was used to explain China's success in getting the epidemic under control and its economy back on track. An assertive social media campaign by a new generation of young Chinese diplomats and a wide range of interviews with senior officials gave this success the necessary visibility. In an essay in *El País*, the South Korean philosopher Byung-Chul Han predicted that 'China will now be able to sell its digital police state as a model of success against the pandemic. China will display the superiority of its system even more proudly.' Less amusing for European decision-makers was that China had a habit of using so-called failures of the West to make its own success stories even shiner. Had the 2008 financial crisis not uncovered the weaknesses of the western capitalist economic model? Did Brexit not show the limits of Europe's cooperative model? And in the same vein: did the high number of COVID casualties in Europe and the US not show the flaws of western democracy and indecisiveness? A battle of narratives, as the EU high representative for foreign affairs called it.

This intensive public diplomacy went hand in hand with generous medical support. In March alone China sent almost four billion face masks all over the world. Other donations included test kits and ventilators. It even deployed Chinese medical personnel. Chinese companies like Alibaba, Huawai and Xiaomi were officially part of this large-scale deployment of mask diplomacy. This makes the link with Chinese economic interests quite clear. Several Chinese companies involved in the medical assistance operations were also important promoters (and beneficiaries) of China's Belt and Road Initiative (BRI), the Chinese project to build global infrastructure like seaports or airports to strengthen Chinese trade connections. On the receiving end, countries that benefited from China's medical support were potential partners in the BRI or in China's broader policy of economic diplomacy. Not much new here. The fact that Alibaba co-founder Jack Ma promised to deliver test kits and face masks to all 54 African countries was just an extension of the Jack Ma Foundation which had been launched in

December 2014 to finance education, entrepreneurship and women's leadership throughout Africa. Another important area of focus was the EU's backyard. Much attention was paid to a group of countries that were part of the '17+1' cooperation format, a Chinese initiative that linked China with twelve central and eastern EU countries and five Western Balkan countries. Serbia especially was well-treated by Beijing.

Some observers think that China's public diplomacy efforts during the COVID-19 crisis are part of a broader ambition to kick the US off the throne of global leadership. This is too far-fetched. Despite China's best efforts, the world is not waiting for Chinese global leadership, and China itself is most likely not looking for it. The Chinese government already has a lot on its plate. It has to manage a population of 1.4 billion people, almost a fifth of the world population (18%). It has to run an economy that is slowing down and at the same time tackle the problem that between now and 2030 its working age population will decline by 73 million. It is also confronted with a series of political challenges, like Hong Kong, Taiwan, vocal minorities on its territory as well as a population increasingly worried about air pollution and environmental degradation. On top of all that, it has to keep an eye on its powerful neighbours such as India, Japan, Indonesia and South Korea. China will surely think twice before it takes on the global leadership role that the US has performed since World War II.

What is more important for China is that no one can thwart its goals, both in its direct geographical sphere of interest and in the pursuit of its economic interests. The latter explains China's desire to increase its influence in the existing multilateral institutions. When you can push the right buttons there, it is easier to shape global rules to suit your own interests. A good example is the International Telecommunications Union, one of the four out of fifteen UN agencies that is now led by a Chinese official for the first time. International UN-backed telecoms standards that strengthen the role of the state and dilute freedom of expression would for sure be in China's interest. Generally, China seems more interested in these kinds of opportunities to shape international norms directly linked to its interests, rather than to run the entire global order. But even if you are just norm shaping you still need friends and networks. China's COVID-19 diplomacy was intended to take care of that.

US-CHINESE RIVALRY, MULTILATERALISM ON THE DEFENSIVE

While the US stumbled backwards and China fell over itself to impress, US-Chinese tensions reached a new level of intensity. They had already been soaring high for about a decade before COVID-19. In the early 2010s the intense economic cooperation between the two that had started in the late seventies gradually came to a head. Between 1978 and 2012 both were able and willing to play down their ideological differences and strategic rivalries, leading to a web of strong economic and commercial relations. American companies invested heavily in China, and large cohorts of Chinese students – some 360,000 a year – brushed up their knowledge in American high schools and universities. But rapid economic growth made China more ambitious and self-confident. Already during the Obama presidency, US presence in the South China Sea had started to become bothersome. With president Trump in the White House, tensions with China became a recurring topic. They even led to a twenty-month trade war between June 2018 and January 2020, when a first agreement was found to lower trade tariffs. As described in the first chapter, the COVID-19 crisis sharpened the tensions to the point where observers started to talk about a new Cold War. That might be a stretch, but the trend of 'de-coupling' continued, at different levels, from businesses and traders to tourists and students. This inevitably made a multilateral response to the COVID-19 crisis much more difficult. Multilateralism had been under pressure for several years. COVID-19 confirmed this trend and probably accelerated it. It was a rather pessimistic UN secretary-general António Guterres who on 26 March in the BBC programme Hardtalk stated that the relationship between the biggest powers has never been as dysfunctional.

When the world's major powers are not on speaking terms, then the UN Security Council, the world's main crisis manager, is paralysed. That was the case during the Cold War, when the US and the USSR were in opposite camps. Most decisions crashed because the other vetoed them, pushing the Security Council into virtual irrelevance. It was only after the fall of the Berlin Wall that the Council became a crucial player in the field of international peace and security. But during the COVID-19 crisis the Security Council struggled to be of use. The 2014 Ebola outbreak showed us that the Council could play a useful role. In September of that year the Security Council was discussing a public health crisis for the first time in its almost 70-year history. Under the leadership of the United States (as it happens), it unanimously approved a resolution that declared the spread of the Ebola virus in Liberia, Sierra Leone and Guinea a 'threat to international peace and security'. It also called on the world community to send more healthcare assistance to the three African countries. The resolution had no fewer than 130 co-sponsors, a unique show of worldwide solidarity.

The contrast with the COVID-19 crisis could hardly be

more apparent. It took more than three months after the outbreak of the virus before the Security Council even held its first videoconference on the topic, on 9 April. By then 87,000 people had died and the virus had spread to more than 180 countries. The Security Council meeting came shortly after the UN secretary-general had called for an immediate ceasefire in all corners of the globe, in all conflicts. Only when weapons were downed could aid reach those that needed it. 'There should be only one fight in our world today, our shared battle against COVID19', he argued. It would have been a strong signal if the Security Council supported this call.

But instead of a joint commitment to fight the pandemic, it showed its division. A Franco-Tunisian draft resolution on COVID-19 ended up in a bitter fight between the US and China. After weeks of intense negotiations, the US continued to block the resolution because of a (very implicit) reference to the World Health Organization. A compromise proposal stressed 'the urgent need to support all countries, as well as all relevant entities of the United Nations system, including specialized health agencies (…) to enhance coordination and assist in the global fight against COVID-19.' But even the term 'specialized health agencies' went too far for the US, who were increasingly at loggerheads with the WHO. The US also wanted to include an explicit reference on how the pandemic started, which China refused. A pretty sad soap storyline that dragged on for weeks and weeks.

It was not just the WHO and the UN Security Council that were on shaky ground. The G20 was another multilateral forum that, with the two fighting cocks at the same table, provided less leadership than in the previous crisis. In the 2008-2010 global financial crisis this group of the nineteen richest countries and the EU was key. World leaders discussed the economic challenges at their Summit meetings in 2008 in Washington, in 2009 in London and Pittsburgh and in 2010 in Toronto. In Pittsburgh, all major global institutions that could help tackle the economic crisis joined in, from the IMF and the World Bank to the World Trade Organization and the Association of Southeast Asian Nations. These meetings resulted in $500 billion of extra firepower for the International Monetary Fund to preserve global financial stability and put pressure on countries not to resort to protectionist measures, since these would have only made the crisis worse. This was true international cooperation in action. Right now, the economic challenges are probably bigger than they were then. According to the IMF, the world has entered a recession. The International Labour Organization warned that the crisis could wipe out 195 million jobs globally in the second quarter of 2020 alone. Yet, opinions within the G20 now seem further apart than they were ten years ago.

The other important 'G' forum, the G7, also functioned less efficiently than it should. The G7 Summit on 16 March, with the US as acting Chair, did not lead to any concrete results. A month earlier the G7 foreign ministers failed to reach an agreement because of the US' insistence on language that subtly referred to China as being responsible for the outbreak of the pandemic. A proposal that all other participants – Japan, Italy, France, the UK, Germany and Canada – shot down immediately.

In many ways, the COVID-19 crisis confirmed the direction in which the global order had been evolving for some years. This of course has an important impact on the European Union. That impact was, in my opinion, accurately summarised by commissioner Thierry Breton, in a video-conference with the European industry ministers on 24 March: 'We cannot count on anybody but only ourselves. We need to walk alone'. Brutal, shocking perhaps, but at least someone had named the elephant in the room.

In the last two or three years others had come to the same conclusion, but they packaged it in more diplomatic language. In a memorable speech in the auditorium of the Sorbonne University in Paris in September 2017 president Macron declared that the 'only way to ensure our future, is the rebuilding of a sovereign, united and democratic Europe.' Four months earlier, chancellor Merkel had told a busy beer hall rally in Bavaria that 'the days when Europe could rely on others were over', clearly referring to the US. And in his 2018 State of the Union, European Commission president Juncker reworded it as follows: 'The geopolitical situation makes this Europe's hour: the time for European sovereignty has come. It is time Europe took its destiny into its own hands.' *Weltpolitikfähigkeit*, he called it.

So how to shape that *Weltpolitikfähigkeit*? In any case it is in Europe's interest that this sovereignty is outward-looking instead of inward-looking, and based on strategic partnerships. It was clear throughout the COVID crisis that this remains the preferred option of the EU. The EU was amongst those who permanently argued in favour of a multilateral global response to the COVID-19 crisis.

When on 8 April the EU published a plan on how to react globally to the pandemic, international cooperation was the common thread running through the text: 'We are taking a leadership role in the coordination efforts undertaken by the United Nations, the G20, the G7 (…) The EU will put its full weight behind the UN Secretary General's efforts to coordinate a UN-wide response.'

In total, the EU set aside almost €35 billion to help its partner countries fight the virus. A considerable chunk of this money, as well as a large part of the EU's humanitarian aid, went to Africa and Europe's immediate Balkan neighbours, two regions of tremendous priority to the Union. Even though the pandemic forced the EU to focus much time and energy on keeping its own head above water, the EU kept investing in both regions. In early May, the Zagreb Summit brought the EU institutions, almost all European leaders and the leaders of the Western Balkan countries together in a joint videoconference. The host, Croatian prime minister Plenković summarised as follows: 'These countries [of the Western Balkan] are in a way surrounded by the EU. If we look at the geography, there is nowhere else they could go'. As far as Africa was concerned, two days after the successful Summit with the Western Balkans, the EU launched an EU Humanitarian Air Bridge to transport humanitarian workers and emergency supplies to countries in need of assistance. Africa was clearly being prioritised. The first flight left on 8 May. Destination: Central African Republic. By early July, it had flown more than 350 billion tons of essential humanitarian and medical material to countries in need.

The EU also played a very active role in the G20. At the 26 March videoconference of G20 leaders, Ursula von der Leyen and Charles Michel stressed the 'pivotal role of the G20 in ensuring global coordination'. They announced their intention to host a virtual pledging conference on 4

May. In three hours of live and recorded video messages by world leaders, that event, called 'Coronavirus Global Response', raised almost €7.5 billion to accelerate research on vaccines and to produce and deploy test kits and therapeutic material for those countries that needed it most. Not all the money raised was new cash, but the fact that the world united to fight the virus sent a strong symbolic signal. That was the message that Ursula von der Leyen wanted to give: 'Today the world showed extraordinary unity for the common good. Governments and global health organizations joined forces against coronavirus.' The world, *minus* the two countries who declined the invite: Russia, and… the United States. A G-zero world indeed.

CHAPTER 13

The Need for EU 'Strategic Autonomy'

- What strategic autonomy really means
- How the EU can become less dependent on China and other nations
- Why the EU should take a very close look at some foreign investors

MULTIPLE DEPENDENCY

In one area in particular the COVID-19 crisis was a rough wake-up call for the EU. It showed how dependent the European Union's economy was on others, mainly China. In the beginning of the crisis Europe kept a close eye on China's partial lockdown. Chinese factories started to produce less because a large part of the Chinese workforce was in quarantine. Lockdown measures hindered traffic so it was more difficult for trucks to bring goods to Chinese ports destined for Europe. Many of those products were raw materials or intermediate goods. The latter are used to make other goods, in Europe. After all, China accounts for a fifth of global trade in intermediate products, such as LCD screens for TVs produced in Poland or vital parts needed for fridges produced in Germany. There was no immediate cause for concern, but if China's lockdown lasted several weeks, European companies might have to close down too. A TV isn't much use without a screen.

When the epidemic reached Europe there was a more short-term reason to be worried: the EU's dependency on China and India for medicines and medical equipment. European Commission vice-president Věra Jourová even called it a 'morbid dependency'. While Europe is still one of the top manufacturers of drugs, the active pharmaceutical ingredients (API) that are needed to produce these medicines are in most cases imported from India or China. It is cheaper to produce these ingredients there than in Europe. Right now, China has a 20% market share of the global production of such ingredients, making it the biggest single provider. For some products, such as most of our antibiotics or painkillers like ibuprofen, Chinese companies control even 90% of the API market. If something goes wrong in those Chinese or Indian factories, you can expect shortages in Europe.

The EU was well aware of this risk. In the summer of 2018, the Netherlands was confronted with major shortages of the contraceptive pill, mainly because of production errors in Chinese and Indian factories. In June 2019, a Polish newspaper reported shortages of certain life-saving medicines after tens of Chinese factories were closed down in a bid to combat pollution. And in France, in the autumn of 2018, it was increasingly difficult for Parkinson's patients to get their medicines. This inspired the French health minister Agnès Buzyn to address the growing shortages. One of her proposals was to 'relocalize the production of APIs and medicines to France and to Europe'. The COVID-19 outbreak moved the issue considerably higher on the list of priorities. Even more so when Europe's dependency on China for other medical supplies, such as face masks, became painfully apparent. The medical sector was not the only one in which Europe's dependency was laid bare. Technology was another. If it had not been for COVID and mandatory teleworking it would probably have been another year before I discovered Zoom or would become a daily user of Teams (Microsoft), WebEx (Cisco) or even Houseparty. These tools got an enormous boost during the pandemic. Zoom Video grew during the crisis from 10 million active users in late 2019 to more than 300 million in April 2020. By then the Chinese internet giant Tencent had also rolled out its videoconferencing app VooV in more than 100 countries. With a capacity that allows up to 300 people to participate in one online meeting, VooV is a serious competitor for California-based Zoom.

So where is Europe in all this? The Belgian consultant Econopolis recently gave an interesting overview of the players that dominate the technology market. Bear with me here while I quote what they found out: 'The biggest Cloud providers are Amazon, Microsoft, Google and Alibaba (3x US, 1x Asia). The biggest chip producers are TSMC, Samsung and Intel (2x Asia, 1x US). The biggest Gaming Software companies are Tencent, Nintendo, NetEase, Activision Blizzard, EA, Take Two, Ubisoft and CD Project (3x Asia, 3x US, 2x Europe). The biggest cybersecurity companies are Palo Alto, Fortinet, Check Point (3x US/Israel). The biggest Digital Payments companies are Visa, Mastercard, Alex, Paypal, Alipay, Tencent, Unipay, Adyen (4x US, 3x Asia, 1x Europe). The biggest Semiconductor Equipment companies: Applied Materials, Lam Research, KLA Tencor, ASM-Litho, Tokyo Electron, ASM Pacific, Kulicke & Soffa (4x US, 2x Asia, 1x Europe). The biggest 5G players: Huawei, ZTE, Qualcom, Mediatek, Nokia, Ericsson, Samsung, TSMC (5x Asia, 2x Europe, 1x US). And the biggest Robotica companies: Keyence, Fanuc, Yaskawa, Cognex (3x Asia, 1x US).' The list is not even complete, but I think you get the idea. If the digital economy drives the total economy, then the

EU needs to up its game in the next twenty years compared to the last thirty. China has explicitly identified global leadership in technologies such as Artificial Intelligence, batteries, 5G and Big Data as one of its national security and economic objectives. Global leadership that will definitely spill over into the geopolitical sphere, all the more so since many of the Chinese companies are national champions, with very close links to the Chinese authorities and with sufficient financial means to invest worldwide, including in Europe.

Europe had to come up with an answer. That answer was called: 'strategic autonomy'.

THE QUEST FOR STRATEGIC AUTONOMY

In this field too the COVID pandemic was merely a catalyst, an accelerator. In certain sectors of the economy quite some work had been done to make the EU less dependent on other countries. A good example are the efforts made in the last ten years by the European Commission to drastically reduce Europe's dependency on imported energy. Importing energy is not only expensive, it also makes Europe dependent on one single supplier and thus vulnerable. That's what happened in January 2009, when state-owned Russian gas company Gazprom turned the tap off in Europe. The reason was a Russian-Ukrainian dispute; the result was a long, cold winter for many households in central and eastern Europe. This triggered new European legislation to make the EU less energy dependent.

Another example is the EU's investment in Galileo. Europe's economy will be ever more dependent on satellite navigation for everything from automated driving to monitoring pollution or land use. Yet, before Galileo, European users fully depended on the American GPS system or on Russian GLONASS satellites. But those days are gone. With Galileo, the EU now has its own independent satellite navigation system.

The COVID outbreak now gives the EU another reason to become more independent (or 'autonomous') in other key sectors. And this is what strategic autonomy – or 'economic sovereignty' as chancellor Merkel and president Macron called it – is all about. As French finance minister Bruno Le Maire put it: 'There will be a 'before' and an 'after' the coronavirus [outbreak] in global economics. We have to decrease our dependency on a couple of large powers, in particular China, for the supply of certain products and strengthen our sovereignty in strategic value chains, like cars, aerospace and medicines.' In other words: let's diversify our sources of supply and, whenever possible, go for 'Made in Europe'. The goods and services that we really need should be produced in Europe.

KEEP WHAT YOU HAVE AND GET BACK WHAT YOU LOST

To make sure that essential products are produced in the European Union, the first logical step is to keep hold of the companies that are already active here. Easier said than done. In March it became clear that European health tech companies had caught the eye of foreign buyers. On 15 March, the German government revealed that US president Trump offered a large sum of money to the German biotech company CureVac to move its research facility to the US. The company was working on a coronavirus vaccine and the US was eager to secure exclusive rights to it. To keep the company in Germany, the German government stepped in and became a shareholder. The EU, through the European Investment Bank, also offered the company a €75 million investment to continue to develop the vaccine in Europe.

But this is only the tip of the iceberg. There is a real risk that the economic fall-out of the crisis has foreign bargain hunters snapping up innovative European companies, most of which are small or medium-sized companies. With shares falling to record lows, they could easily fall into the hands of rich Chinese investors or sovereign wealth funds from the Gulf region (a bit like Belgian football teams). It isn't really a level playing field. European companies need money while state-supported or even state-owned Chinese companies are being flooded by government money. But if China and others take control of European technologies or infrastructure, it will not only make the recovery of Europe's economy harder, it can also create security risks. Do we really want critical energy or telecom infrastructure in Chinese hands? The answer is obvious.

Europe knew all too well what these risks were well before the COVID outbreak. When in 2016 the Chinese company Medea took over the German robot producer KuKa, Germany sounded the alarm (too late for KuKa though). Since then the topic has the EU's attention. In an unusually undiplomatic reflection paper on EU-China relations, written by the European Commission and the European External Action Service in March 2019, the screening of foreign investments was an important issue.

A month later the EU agreed on a better way to defend the EU's strategic interests against foreign investors. The idea was pretty simple. If a country was approached by a foreign investor interested in, say, energy, communications, data, space, finance, ports or airports, it was encouraged to share that information with other countries and with the Commission. The Commission could give its opinion, but could not stop the investment. The final decision lay with the country. Apart from this, the countries would also help each other to set up national mechanisms to screen foreign investments. This new way of working would come into force in October 2020.

By then it could be too late for many companies. The European Commission did not just want to sit back and wait. In March 2020 it came with extra 'guidance concerning Foreign Direct Investments and protection of Europe's strategic assets', mainly to draw the countries' attention to the risk of selling their companies. Europe was not for sale, was the motto. The Commission also buried one of its taboos to help governments protect their companies. If the only way to prevent a take-over was for a government to buy stakes in 'their' companies and thus become co-owner, then so be it. 'We don't have any issues of states acting as market participants if need be – if they provide shares in a company, if they want to prevent a takeover of this kind', Margrethe Vestager, one of the leading vice-presidents of the European Commission told *The Financial Times* mid-April. This is remarkable. The Commission had never been a big fan of state intervention in private companies. But when push came to shove, it started to show more flexibility.

Some EU countries did not hang about either. Germany adopted a law in April with the mouthful of a name *Aussenwirtschaftsgesetz*, making foreign take-overs much more difficult. France took a similar decision and explicitly included the food sector and – in a very smart move – media companies. And in the European Parliament Manfred Weber, the German leader of the European People's Party even asked for a 12-month freeze on any Chinese take-overs of undervalued European companies. COVID-19 was the lighter fuel to a debate that been smouldering for some time.

Keeping the companies in European hands, in Europe, is one thing. But the COVID-19 crisis showed that this was not enough. What was needed was a genuine European industrial strategy which would also bring back certain sectors of manufacturing to the EU. This so-called 're-shoring' would be particularly relevant in some strategic sectors such as robotics, blockchain and microelectronics. And let's not forget medical products and pharmaceuticals.

When the European Commission presented its *New Industrial Strategy for Europe* on 10 March all these ideas, including the one on strategic autonomy, were included. Several countries welcomed it, but overall reactions were lukewarm. The much-read journal *Politico* was even outspokenly negative: 'Brussels is reheating a heap of leftovers from previous economic plans, and hoping that a generous dollop of political willpower will finally make them a roaring success on the sixth serving'.

Six industrial strategies in fifteen years is indeed too much of a good thing. The number of new ideas is not infinite, nor is the capacity to deliver. When the 2014 strategy was presented, under the not so modest title *Towards an Industrial Renaissance,* I was at the cabinet of president Van Rompuy. I could see first-hand that amongst the European leaders there was, with two or three exceptions, clearly no appetite to discuss this topic. A European Council session scheduled to explicitly discuss industrial policy, in February 2014, was cancelled, even though French president Hollande had been asking for it for more than a year. When the topic was finally discussed a month later, re-shoring manufacturing to Europe emerged as one of the key goals. But not much had happened since then. On the contrary.

WILL IT BE DIFFERENT THIS TIME?

Much has changed since 2014. The perception of the manufacturing industry has changed dramatically. Back in 2014, the main focus was on services, which accounted for almost 70% of the European GDP. Industry was in decline. It mainly offered repetitive, monotonous and underpaid jobs that were moving outside Europe anyway. Right now, such a distinction no longer makes much sense. The digital world has blurred the lines. A modern car is software on wheels. This idea was well captured by Klaus Schwab, founder and chairman of the World Economic Forum. In 2016 he launched the concept of The Fourth Industrial Revolution. Industry is all about technology, data and creativity. An Industrial Internet of Things is developing, with computers and machines all being interconnected. When I visited the Lego Factory in Billund, Denmark, the CEO's summary of their production process opened my eyes: 'The first time a human being touches the lego bricks, is when a child opens the box'. The factory felt like a spaceship: robots, self-driving carts, and just one supervisor. Industry is not something of the past. It has just been reinvented.

Thanks to new technologies, re-shoring is no longer a distant reality. When the American futurologist Jeremy Rifkin introduced me to the Rotterdam-The Hague Metropolitan Area, a whole new world opened up. He gave one concrete example: the development of a 3D printing field lab that prints spare and replacement parts for ships in the Port of Rotterdam. Currently, it takes months to make and transport those parts. They are usually produced in China. This 3D technology makes it possible to produce them on the spot in Rotterdam, giving the port a competitive advantage. In late November 2019, the lab manufactured the world's very first 3D-printed ship's propeller: 400 kilograms of 'Made in Europe' innovation. Another leap of progress since 2014 is that the European Commission has moved its focus from general targets ('the share of industry in European GDP should be 20% by 2020') to very tangible transnational projects. A good example is the European Battery Alliance, launched in October 2017 by Commission vice-president Šefčovič. Batteries are crucial for a greener economy based on renewable energy and electric mobility. But the EU is (too) dependent on third countries like China for the production of battery cells. That's where the Battery Alliance comes in. It brings together researchers, production companies and financing by governments and European institutions. If all goes well, a first production site should be up and running in early 2021 in Sweden and by 2022 in Germany and France. A similar push will also be given to other promising technologies in the field of hydrogen, through the launch of the Clean Hydrogen Alliance. These kinds of concrete projects, in EU jargon 'Important Projects of Common European Interest', pave the way for other strategic industries in the EU, including in healthcare or Artificial Intelligence. The next time Europe is hit by a health crisis, maybe it will be 3D-printing its own face masks and exporting them to others in need.

TIME TO TACKLE SOME TOUGH QUESTIONS

When it comes to industrial policy, COVID-19 has created a momentum that in previous years simply did not exist. By exposing the EU's huge dependency on (mainly) China, it touched a sensitive ideological nerve. For the French commissioner Thierry Breton, it showed that Europe may have gone too far in globalisation. Strategic autonomy, or economic sovereignty as France and Germany prefer, is indeed part of the solution. But only if two conditions are met.

Firstly, building on what was said in the previous chapter, economic sovereignty should be outward-looking. Becoming less economically vulnerable does not mean becoming autarchic. The screening of foreign investments is a good example. The EU is the main destination for foreign direct investment in the world. At the end of 2017 this created some 16 million jobs. The goal is to avoid key assets being sold out, not banning foreign investments entirely. In the same vein, reducing the EU's over-reliance on China in *certain* strategic sectors does not mean becoming self-sufficient in *all* sectors. And protection does not necessarily mean protectionism.

This is important. Globalisation brings benefits in many different areas, from generating economic growth to halving child mortality. At the same time, the COVID-19 pandemic showed that some elements of it deserve at least a question mark, specifically the chains of production. Does it make sense that components travel halfway around the globe before being assembled in Europe? Is it sustainable to develop lithium (or other raw materials) in Europe, just for it to be shipped over to Asia to be refined there before then being sent back to Europe? Can we still rely on 'just-in-time' manufacturing, whereby components or goods are delivered at the last minute? And do we really need Argentinian steak with all those cows we have in Europe? European companies need foreign markets and foreign companies need the European market. But this does not mean that certain practices should not be questioned.

Secondly, a strong – perhaps stronger – EU is crucial in this area. When at the outset of the crisis India introduced an export ban on paracetamol and other medical ingredients, it only lifted this ban (at least partially) after long negotiations with the European Commission. Maybe a few EU countries can go head to head with India, but the majority of smaller ones do not have that same leverage. Similarly, some decisions are better off being made by Europe as a whole. One example: does it make sense in a Union in which all the economies are closely interlinked that each country individually decides whether or not to allow foreign investments in sensitive areas? Or would this kind of decision be better taken by the Council, on the advice of the Commission and the high representative for foreign affairs? Right now, about half of EU countries have a screening mechanism in place, often very different ones. Wouldn't some harmonisation or coordination be far more efficient?

And finally, hasn't the time come to decide on whether or not to change the rules of the game and enable European champions to emerge? Some argue that Europe needs companies that are big enough to compete on the global market. Others warn against the impact these champions will have on smaller European businesses, innovation and – not in the least – consumers. In 2019 the Commission still blocked a merger between Siemens and Alstom, which would have created a European champion. The COVID-19 crisis put the question back on the table. In short: there is still a long way to go. But now is the time to take bold decisions and move forward.

CHAPTER 14

The European Way of Life

- Why one European app to fight the virus is an illusion
- How COVID-19 can be a threat to our fundamental rights
- Why Asian solutions don't necessarily work in Europe

The COVID-19 pandemic was a nightmare on many fronts. The human costs were very high, the socio-economic costs overwhelming. But there is another front that is equally important: the risk that the virus infects the foundations of our democracies, and the rule of law and fundamental freedoms on which they are based.

In several countries around the globe basic freedoms were restricted in a way that would have been unthinkable just a few months ago. Governments armed themselves against the virus with emergency laws and special powers. Some countries declared a state of emergency. This was necessary of course. Without strict lockdown measures the catastrophic impact would have been even bigger.

But restricting the freedom of citizens is not without risks. The V-Dem Institute of the University of Gothenburg found that democracies are 75% more likely to erode under a state of emergency. In a state of emergency, power typically becomes more centralised. It shifts to the government which rules by decree; for parliaments it becomes more difficult to play their overseeing role; in some places the state having a bigger say in the economy combined with more emergency funding increases the risk of corruption; fundamental rights such as freedom of the press come under pressure. It is often a matter of keeping things in proportion. Social distancing measures inevitably restricted freedom of movement and freedom of assembly. The question is: where to draw the line? When on 18 April the city of Stuttgart simply said 'no' to a 50-person demonstration against the German lockdown, Germany's Federal Constitutional Court rapped the city's knuckles: Stuttgart should have allowed a lower number of participants observing the correct physical distancing measures. In other words: governments should do their utmost to combat the virus without completely abandoning essential human rights.

The challenge is real: the V-Dem Institute I just referred to found that during the COVID-19 crisis 48 countries around the world showed a high risk of democratic decline, while 34 were at medium risk, including the US (while I was writing this chapter, US president Donald Trump announced an executive order to limit the power of social media companies, as it happened just after Twitter fact-checked two of his tweets). In an online debate organised by the European think tank Friends of Europe, justice commissioner Didier Reynders summarised the challenge as follows: 'We enter the crisis with a democracy and with a respect for our values. We need to go out of the crisis with the same democracy and with the same capacity to protect the values'. Even in times of crisis, the rule of law had to be upheld.

Interestingly enough, here too COVID-19 seemed to accelerate a trend that was not new. Countries with a limited democratic immune system proved especially vulnerable. According to the World Justice Project, their number had increased in recent years. In its 2020 Index it found that respect for the rule of law continued to weaken worldwide: 'The declines were widespread and seen in all corners of the world.' The 2017 Democracy Index of the Economist Intelligence Unit registered the worst year for global democracy since 2010-11. And the 2020 World Press Freedom Index by Reporters without Borders found a clear correlation between suppression of freedom of the press in response to the coronavirus pandemic, and a country's ranking in the Index. The pandemic gave authoritarian governments an excuse, an opportunity, and sometimes even the means, to impose measures that would be much more difficult or even impossible under normal circumstances.

The European Union is no exception. Within the Union respect for the rule of law is based on one of the most important parts of the European Treaty, Article 2. It is worth quoting it in full: 'The Union is founded on the values of respect for human dignity, freedom, democracy, equality, the rule of law and respect for human rights, including the rights of persons belonging to minorities.' In previous years, these principles were repeatedly challenged from within. Even before the COVID pandemic broke out, two countries were put under closer scrutiny: Hungary and Poland, a pair that faced heavy criticism for undermining the rule of law in their country.

In the case of Hungary, the criticism goes back to the early 2010s, when the government of Viktor Orbán made several changes to the Hungarian Constitution. The objective was to further strengthen the power of the government. For media outlets and non-governmental organisations which were critical towards the government it became more difficult to function. The Central European University, sponsored by billionaire and Orbán critic Georges

Soros, came under intense pressure and ended up moving part of its operations from Budapest to Vienna. Prime minister Orbán's outspoken position on migration and his defence of an 'illiberal democracy' as an alternative to Western liberal democracy did not win him any friends in mainstream and liberal European circles (which he didn't mind anyway). The same goes for Poland. Criticism was on the rise since 2015 when the Law and Justice Party won an outright majority in the parliamentary elections. The government's decisions to have more direct control over the judiciary as well as its restrictive policies on LGBT+ rights did not go unnoticed in Brussels.

If there are strong indications or if a serious risk that a country violates the fundamental values of the EU, then the European Union can invoke Article 7 of the Treaty. A so-called Article 7 procedure can be launched by the Commission, the European Parliament or one third of the countries. If that happens the Commission investigates and makes recommendations that are discussed by the countries in the form of hearings. The procedure can result in sanctions. A country can even lose its right to vote. After a two-year dialogue with Poland, the Commission launched an Article 7 procedure in 2017. The main straw that broke the camel's back was Poland's attempts to bring the judicial branch under governmental control. A year later, the European Parliament asked for an Article 7 procedure to be launched for Hungary.

During the COVID-19 crisis it was precisely these two countries that came under fire a couple of times. The fact that on 11 March the Orbán government declared a 'state of danger' as they called it, was not so unusual. The government shut down universities, closed schools and banned large gatherings, just like many other European governments were doing around that time. But what really raised eyebrows was the adoption of a 'Bill on the

Protection against the Coronavirus' three weeks later. Several rule of law defenders were shocked by the lack of an expiry date on the bill. Other countries deploying special powers usually set a clear end date. In Belgium, the government's special powers were for three months, extendable by another three months. In Norway the government had to go back to parliament every month if it wanted to extend the emergency regime. But in the case of Hungary this 'rule by decree' would continue until the parliament, in which the government relied on a solid two-thirds majority, decided otherwise. There literally was no end in sight.

The state of danger also gave the Hungarian government more repressive firepower. Anyone who did not respect the rules of quarantine faced a prison sentence of up to five years. And every person who published false or distorted facts that could agitate public opinion could also be sent to jail for up to five years. A decision that of course was very sensitive in a country where freedom of the press had been under pressure for several years. Bulgaria, ranked 111th in terms of press freedom in the Reporters Without Borders 2020 edition of the World Press Freedom Index, took a similar measure. But this got far less attention.

The Hungarian government was quick to defend its state of danger. Zoltán Kovács, the Hungarian secretary of state for public diplomacy and relations, pointed at other EU countries with 'similar' provisions, such as Belgium and France. Sweden, which temporarily granted extraordinary powers to the government and reduced the number of its parliamentarians, was also put in the same basket. Hungary also tried to justify its actions by referring to the European Commission, which had itself repeatedly stressed the importance of the fight against disinformation. But this did not stop the criticism, including in Orbán's own political family. A letter written by thirteen party leaders belonging to Orbán's European People's Party (EPP) on 2 April left little unsaid: 'We fear that Prime Minister Orbán will use this newly achieved power to further extend the government's grip on civil society (…) We call on the expulsion of Fidesz [the party of Prime Minister Orbán] from the EPP. We furthermore underline our support for the European Commission and call on joint action by the Member States to address the situation in Hungary forcefully.' EPP president Donald Tusk was equally outspoken. He called the developments politically dangerous and morally unacceptable.

Some (mainly Western European) countries decided to react with a short joint declaration in which their foreign ministers once again expressed their commitment to the rule of law: 'In this unprecedented situation it is legitimate that Member States adopt extraordinary measures to protect their citizens and overcome the crisis. We are however deeply concerned about the risk of violations of the principles of Rule of Law, democracy and freedom rights arising from the adoption of certain emergency measures.' The ministers explicitly referred to freedom of expression and freedom of the press, but not to Hungary. The process leading up to the declaration was in fact rather messy. Several countries, mainly from the eastern part of Europe, had not been consulted on the initiative, leading to bitter reactions from their side. The Hungarian minister, supported by Poland, defended the Hungarian law, and stated – rather tersely – that it could fully subscribe to everything that was said in the declaration. It offered to be part of it, which of course is hard to refuse. In the final version, Hungary figures prominently in the list of subscribers.

The Commission was more explicit. One day after Hungary had adopted its emergency law, von der Leyen issued a statement reminding all countries that 'the European Union is founded on the values of freedom, democracy, the rule of law and respect for human rights. (...) We must uphold and defend them, even in these challenging times.' But it was mainly Rule of Law Commission vice-president Jourová, a liberal from the Czech Republic, who did not mince her words. With an explicit reference to the Hungarian prime minister she said: 'Mr. Orbán will have to prove that our concerns are unfounded'. She also hinted at financial sanctions: 'Now we have a chance, in the new budget negotiations, to keep this conditionality alive (...) To be blunt, I think that if somebody does not understand our values, they should understand the value of money'. This was a reference to the Commission's proposal for the new Multiannual Financial Framework, which included a clause on rule of law conditionality: if a country does not sufficiently respect the rule of law, the EU could suspend, reduce or restrict access to EU funding. A serious stick to use.

In early June, when the virus was under control in Hungary, the government formally withdrew the state of danger. Justice minister Varga had her own take on the entire episode: Hungary had been subject to 'an unprecedented, coordinated political campaign and hysteria for months', she said. The fact that after two months the state of emergency came to an end was the best proof, in her opinion, that it had always been designed as a temporary measure.

During the COVID-19 crisis, Poland too was a cause for concern in Brussels. The main reason here was the Polish decision to go ahead with the presidential elections, despite the outbreak of the pandemic and the rules on social distancing. The ruling Law and Justice Party was determined to have these elections as planned, on 10 May. This was pretty exceptional. No fewer than eight EU countries cancelled their (local) elections during the pandemic. Outside Europe, many other countries did the same, from Ethiopia to Serbia to Sri Lanka.

The Polish opposition parties were not amused. They argued that it was impossible to have a proper election campaign while the country was fighting a pandemic. Not having a campaign would be a huge advantage for the re-election hopes of president Duda. Since he was closely involved in managing the COVID crisis, he was assured of much visibility, they argued. Without a proper campaign the opposition did not have that advantage. But the government went full steam ahead. To make sure that the elections could take place on 10 May it decided to run them by postal vote. There would be no physical polling stations. This too raised serious concerns. Would all Poles, including those living abroad, have a chance to vote? And what about data protection, since the postal services, of which the Polish Treasury was the sole shareholder, needed personal data to prepare the elections? Despite these concerns, the government pushed the necessary legislative changes through parliament.

For the European Commission, this was teetering on another attempt to erode the rule of law in Poland. Just after the decision on postal voting was taken, Commission vice-president Jourová declared: 'Corona must be killed, but democracy must survive (…) I am concerned about free and fair elections in the country, about the chance to vote for all candidates, about the ability [of all candidates] to campaign equally.' Her colleague commissioner Didier Reynders echoed these concerns. On 6 May, just four days before the elections and after weeks of uncertainty and confusion, Poland decided to postpone them until June 28. The official reason given was logistics: the elections could no longer be organised in time.

DISINFORMATION AND MISINFORMATION

The fundamental values on which the European Union is based were not only challenged from within. They were also aggressively attacked from outside the EU, on the internet and specifically on social media. The pandemic gave new ammunition to the disinformation campaigns against the EU. These had been going on for some time, often with the involvement of foreign governments.

The Strategic Communication Division of the European External Action Service (the European 'Ministry of Foreign Affairs') carefully monitored the internet for fake news. It hunted for fake anti-EU messages, analysed them and came up with counter-messages. Its inventory gives a good overview of who was behind the campaigns. In many cases it was Russia, to a lesser extent also China. A large portion of the messages portrayed the EU as a divided continent, as a group of democracies unable to handle the COVID-19 crisis. The EU's values were heavily attacked, values that the EU did not follow itself, according to the people behind the campaigns. The EU was selfish, it exaggerated the high mortality rates to strengthen its control over European citizens and did not show solidarity with even its closest allies. The last message here was especially widely distributed in the Western Balkans and throughout Africa.

FOCUS ON:

The European External Action Service (EEAS)

The European External Action Service is the 'foreign ministry' of the European Union. It was created by the Lisbon Treaty and was formally launched on 1 January, 2011. Half of its more than 4000 staff members works in Brussels, the other half in one of the 140 'embassies', called EU delegations. They are the eyes and ears of the EU on the ground.

Not all messages had a geopolitical undertone. Much of the fake information was not disinformation but rather misinformation. That drinking bleach cures the virus or that vodka can be used as hand sanitiser, for instance. Other online campaigns spread conspiracy theories: that 5G telecom masts facilitated the spread of COVID-19, or that most European countries' patient zero was a migrant or refugee, a message that was widely promoted in the far-right 'fascosphere'. Even if such campaigns were not backed-up by a government, they could still be harmful. Anti-5G campaigns triggered vandalism in the Netherlands, Belgium and the UK, while the focus on the migrant community continued to fuel xenophobia, a phenomenon incompatible with the European way of life. Moreover, fake news on medicine became a matter of life or death. Literally.

The European Commission therefore maintained close contacts with the main social media platforms. In its contacts with Facebook, Google and Twitter, it asked them to promote official health information and check or withdraw posts that were proven wrong. The reaction of the platforms was not always as fast and effective as it should have been. After an NGO revealed in mid-April that on average 40% of the Facebook posts that had been debunked by fact-checkers were still online, Facebook boss Mark Zuckerberg announced through gritted teeth: users would receive a message warning them if a COVID-related post they had seen on Facebook, Instagram or WhatsApp contained misinformation. A first step. But the European Commission was clear: if this kind of self-regulation is not sufficient, the EU will come with legislation, forcing the platforms to better monitor online content. That's also the message commissioner Thierry Breton gave Zuckerberg in late May: 'Be careful with our democracy, be careful with disinformation.'

THE FIGHT FOR PRIVACY

The COVID-19 crisis was a stress test for a wide range of fundamental rights, including some less obvious ones. Distance learning put pressure on the right to education, since not all school children had access to a computer or an internet connection. Several countries reported an increase in domestic violence as a result of the lockdown measures. But probably one of the most discussed rights during the pandemic was another one: the right to privacy.

'If the EU had an official religion, it would be privacy', *The Economist* wrote on 23 April. The European Union's image as a champion in the field of data protection was confirmed by their 2018 General Data Protection Regulation ('GDPR'). This legislation sets out the world's strictest data protection rules. It gives European citizens the guarantee that their personal data, from their name and telephone number to their political conviction or trade union membership, will only be used and stored (or not) as they wish. When I buy a book on Amazon in Belgium, Lithuania or Spain, I can be sure that my data cannot be used, stored or sold without my consent. I can ask the company what it uses my data for. I can ask if it sells my profile to other companies that can then bombard me with annoying ads. And I can ask that my data in their database be deleted. And if I delete my Facebook account, I can even demand that it no longer shows up in search engine results. I can request, in other words, to be digitally 'forgotten'. This is not only important for individuals. Since the Cambridge Analytica scandal of early 2018, when it was revealed that the consultancy firm used millions of Facebook users' personal data for political advertising, we also know that data protection is crucial to keep our system of free and fair elections in good shape.

The outbreak of the coronavirus was the first real test where we got to find out just how attached Europe is to the right to privacy in the GDPR era. Several Asian countries had shown that personal data and data-based technologies were instrumental in getting the outbreak under control. The question was whether these technological solutions could also be used in Europe, where privacy rules were much stricter. Let's look at three ways in which data became helpful to fight the pandemic.

Firstly, data technologies can measure the effectiveness of lockdown or social distancing policies. When someone has a mobile phone on them it is relatively easy to determine their location based on the nearest phone mast. When telecom operators give this data to the national authorities, they can easily detect where people are going. Based on such data the Italian authorities found out that in Lombardy, despite the lockdown, 40% of people were still on the move. The authorities used this information to take tougher measures. Other EU countries did the same. Google leant a hand with the info gathering. It used the data it got from smartphones to track the movements of people in 131 countries and made this data publicly available on a website. Its regular 'community mobility reports' show how people react to government measures in a given country or even region. Did people in a certain province do less shopping after the government ordered non-essential shops to close? Did people go to pharmacies and parks more often? Did commuting stay the same? All good to know.

In Europe it is crucial that all this data is anonymous and aggregated (the overall picture, not the individual data). In other words, when my local Belgian police force studies the data, it could not see whether I had, personally, visited another city (or with whom). But it could check if the number of people that stayed in their own city, as required by the measures, went up or down. If the rules were not respected, it could send a police patrol to that area. In some countries, like Belgium, there was hardly any discussion on the use of aggregate telecom data. In other countries, such as Germany, it was much more controversial. Some experts argued that anonymity could never be 100% assured. Someone with access to the raw data could theoretically make a link with a specific individual. If location data pinpointed a person to the same place every night (presumably their house) and to a school ten kilometres away during the day (presumably their job), then you don't have to be a genius to work out who it is. So many were against it that the German government was forced to drop the use of telecom data.

The European Commission saw fewer problems. On 24 March commissioner Thierry Breton asked the CEOs of telecom companies like Deutsche Telekom, Orange or Telecom Italia to share their data with the Commission. The Joint Research Centre, the Commission's scientific body, were ready to start analysis. They could use this information, for instance, to see where medical supplies were most needed. At the end of the crisis all data would be destroyed. The fact that the Commission collected so much data is pretty unique. It also put a huge responsibility on the Commission's shoulders. If the data got hacked, it was the Commission that would be held responsible.

A second way in which data technology was used was to enforce individual quarantine measures. This was of course at the other end of the spectrum from the aggregated data we just saw. Anonymous, aggregated data was not much use here. Instead, individual data was needed. For many Chinese citizens this just became the new way of life early on in the crisis. In some 200 Chinese cities 'Alipay Health' became the must-have app. Every user got a colour code based on a questionnaire and their vital medical statistics, like their body temperature. If you got green you could move around freely and pass all checkpoints in the city. Those with orange had to stay home for seven days. Red meant fourteen days in quarantine. This was the colour nobody wanted because it was the end of your social life: no entry to public transport, taxis, restaurants or even residential buildings.

European governments did not go that far, although Poland did introduce an app to check if people respected the quarantine rules: Home Quarantine. It was launched in mid-April, which made Poland one of the first European countries to use an app in the fight against COVID-19. Polish citizens returning from a trip abroad were obliged to spend two weeks in quarantine. But they got to choose how they wanted to be monitored. The first option was for the police to drop by unannounced. The other was to use the app, which meant regularly submitting geo-tagged selfies which would then be run through face recognition technology. If they failed to post a selfie within 20 minutes of the app requesting it, the police were notified. In several EU countries, this kind of app would be a tough sell.

A third use for the technology was to let someone know if they had crossed paths with someone infected with COVID-19. This form of contact tracing was pretty common in several Asian countries during the pandemic. Some countries went further than others. South Korea was an extreme case. There, health officials used GPS data on someone's mobile phone, CCTV and credit card activity to create a rather intricate map of those infected. If they knew where a COVID patient had been, they warned others who had been in the same area. Everything was made public: the places the patient had visited, the place they lived, the streets they had walked down as well as more personal information, like their year of birth or profession. A South Korean man who spent a fair bit of time in an area known for prostitution made the headlines in several European newspapers warning of the privacy risks involved.

In Europe, this would indeed be unthinkable. Even milder forms of contact tracing were controversial and led to much debate within the EU. Around mid-April it looked like a European-wide tracing app (and one that was in line with all European privacy rules) was in the making. The so-called Pan-European Privacy-Preserving Proximity Tracing (PEPP-PT) project was developed by a group of experts from eight countries. And, true to its acronym, it had people pepped. It was pretty similar to the successful app TraceTogether that was used in Sri Lanka and that got positive press in Europe. The idea was straightforward. When a mobile phone with a PEPP-PT app comes close to another phone with the same app they make a connection using Bluetooth technology ('a Bluetooth handshake'). That contact is stored on the phone itself and stays there for two weeks. When the health authorities are informed by a user that they have the virus, everyone who got one of these handshakes gets a warning. Everything is anonymous: you don't know who you met or where. The only information you get is that you have been close to an infected person. You can then get tested and in turn make sure you don't infect others.

But when it was decided to store the handshake not on the phone itself but on a central platform, the bubble was burst. Several experts pulled out, criticism in the European Parliament increased. On 20 April, a large group of academics published an open letter asking governments to distance themselves from any app with central data storage. From a security and privacy perspective, decentralised storage, on each individual phone, was much safer, they argued. The Dutch privacy watchdog was even more critical: neither centralised nor decentralised storage was 100% anonymous, it warned. It turned out, then, that Europeans care a lot about their privacy, even in the midst of a pandemic.

On 5 May it became clear that a common European position would be very hard to find. The EU's telecom ministers discussed and agreed that an app was useful to complement traditional contract tracing. After all, you don't have the name let alone the phone number of most of the people you meet on the train or in the supermarket. Where a human contact tracer cannot contact them, an app can warn them.

But there was less agreement on the kind of app. A handful of the smaller EU countries were in favour of one single European app. But an overwhelming majority of countries, especially those that already had an app or were close to rolling one out, preferred national apps. As a compromise, they agreed that all apps had to be in line with a set of principles proposed by the European Commission. Data protection and data security were crucial. The app had to be based on anonymity, its use should be voluntary and temporary. Ideally, national health authorities had to be closely involved. For some countries, the national apps needed to be compatible too, especially with summer holidays coming up. If the app of a Dutch tourist in Greece cannot communicate with Greek citizens who live there or French of Lithuanian tourists also on holiday there, contact tracing would be far less effective. In a joint paper in preparation of the ministerial meeting, France, Spain and Italy wrote: 'We acknowledge that different solutions (…) will coexist within the EU. (…) The different choices of each EU country [regarding digital platforms] should all be accepted, and stress that the interoperability between all contact tracing solutions should remain a priority'.

Making sure that all apps could talk to each other was easier said than done. Already in mid-March, France had started to develop a national app. To keep track of how the virus spreads, France wanted to make sure that scientists and policymakers had access to the data. They therefore opted for centralised data storage. The fact that by then the PEPP-PT app did the same and seemed to have the support of the German government made the chances of compatibility more likely. But on 10 April Google and Apple, the company value of which beats that of 30 of the largest German companies on the Frankfurt Exchange, turned the tables. They had partnered up to develop software that radically favoured decentralised apps. Both wanted to prevent governments from getting access to the data, 'in the name of the right of privacy' (oh the irony!). Since their two operating systems Android and iOS dominate 99% of the smart phones market, they were calling the shots. Pragmatic Germany switched sides and moved to a decentralised model. Others like Ireland and Italy followed. On 29 May, Latvia was the first country worldwide to launch an app, Apturi Covid (Stop Covid) that worked on Google and Apple's software. France stuck to its guns. On 3 June, it launched the contract tracing app 'StopCovid', based on a centralised model. Same name but different content. Two weeks later, on 16 June, the German app was launched.

Europe had been put with its backs against the wall. At the end of May, the telecom ministers of France, Germany, Italy, Spain and Portugal expressed their frustration in a joint op-ed. It should be up to democratically elected governments to decide on which tools to develop, not on Silicon Valley. Europe's digital standards should be set 'independently of individual companies', they wrote. But the reality was different. One more example of why Europe's digital sovereignty matters.

CHAPTER 15

Sustainable Recovery

- Why the Commission president said 'This is Europe's moment'
- Why chancellor Merkel will be remembered in European history
- Why the Commission is sticking to its green agenda

'Meeting ended with ministers clapping. press conference in 15 minutes'. With this short tweet, posted at 10:08pm on 9 April, the spokesperson for then Eurogroup president Centeno announced the €540 billion package agreed by the finance ministers. The core of the package was emergency support. Its goal was to keep companies and jobs alive during the darkest moments of the COVID-19 crisis. It was much-needed, short-term life support. But it did not guarantee the patient's rehabilitation. For that, a serious recovery package was needed.

However, the finance ministers had not touched upon the EU's future recovery in their videoconferences. They had exchanged ideas on roughly what a European recovery package might look like. But there had always been one major stumbling block that made a quick agreement impossible. The main bone of contention was not (yet) so much where and to whom the money should go to, but where they were going to find it in the first place. In other words: how to *finance* the recovery of Europe's economy? Once that conundrum was solved, they could talk about how to spend it.

Italy, Spain, France and six other countries had a clear idea on where to find the money: through a 'common debt instrument', as they called it. In other words: borrow it together. To support Europe's economic recovery, a European institution or fund had to borrow money on the market by issuing common European bonds. Investors that buy a European bond lend money to the EU. In return the EU pays interest, as a thank you. When the bond expires, the EU pays the investors back. In the meantime, the EU can use the money for investments in healthcare or socio-economic recovery programmes. These are pretty safe investments. An investor can be quite confident that the EU (having quite some economically strong countries) will come good on its repayments. The risk is low, so the interest rates are low. For a country with a high level of debt, like Italy or Spain, investors might not be so confident, so they would ask a higher interest rate. All in all, these 'eurobonds' would be a much cheaper way for the EU to raise the money. That is what the nine leaders of the countries that came up with the initiative asked for in their joint letter of 25 March to European Council president Michel.

Soon after, they got unexpected support from two European commissioners. On 5 April, French commissioner Thierry Breton and Italian commissioner Paolo Gentiloni (Economy) called for 'Un fondo per la Rinascita', a new fund that would issue common European bonds to fund Europe's 'rebirth'. A day earlier, Spanish prime minister Pedro Sánchez similarly asked for 'a new Marshall Plan' that should be financed by European bonds.

Just one problem, though – Breton and Gentiloni's boss,

Commission president von der Leyen, disagreed. Europe's recovery should not be based on new tricks like corona-bonds, as they were called in the media. They should be able to use the existing European budget, the Multiannual Financial Framework, which leaders were trying to find an agreement on. This is the position she defended in her own op-ed, published a day before that of her commissioners: '[To lift our economy out of the crisis valley] we will need massive investment in the form of a Marshall Plan for Europe', a Marshall Plan that should build on the new Multiannual Financial Framework (MFF). This was also the opinion of German chancellor Angela Merkel. She too had called, ten days earlier, for a 'Marshall Plan-like stimulus strategy' within the Multiannual Financial Framework.

Germany was part of a much larger group of countries – the Netherlands, Finland, Austria, Sweden, Denmark, Estonia – that were strongly opposed to the idea of eurobonds or corona-bonds. If the EU issues eurobonds, the more well-off countries could end up saddled with the debt of the less well-off countries. 'Why should the Netherlands guarantee the debts others make?', the Dutch finance minister argued. In other words, they were afraid of a 'moral hazard': if someone else is picking up the bill, why worry about getting into debt?

So in March 2020, we had time-travelled back to 2012. Back then, during the eurocrisis, the countries with high levels of debt also asked for eurobonds. The others refused, for exactly the same reason. The moment it turned into a discussion about eurobonds or coronabonds, it became highly symbolic. In their 9 April 2020 meeting, the most finance ministers could agree on was captured in the following sentence: 'Subject to guidance from Leaders, discussions on the legal and practical aspects of such a fund, including its relation to the EU budget, its sources of financing and on innovative financial instruments, consistent with EU Treaties, will prepare the ground for a decision'. In other words, the next EU Multiannual Financial Framework had to play a central role in economic recovery (the German line), there was an openness to 'innovative financial instruments' (the Italian line), and all the rest was up for the leaders to decide.

Two weeks later, on 23 April, the European Council kicked the can down the road, to the Commission. It asked the Commission to come up with a proposal for an ambitious recovery fund or a similar instrument, linked in one way or another to an adjusted Multiannual Financial Framework. Most long-term EU observers, at that point, were rather sceptical: eurobonds or a similar common debt approach? Not in their lifetime. But then came Europe's moment.

WINDS OF MAY, THAT DANCE ON THE SEA (JAMES JOYCE)

May 2020 was a remarkable month. It was the month in which the European Union started to reinvent itself.

The first half of the month was uneventful. Europe Day, 9 May, was quieter than in previous years. Normally this is the day when the European institutions open their doors for the public to look around. This year, which also happened to be the 70th anniversary of the Schuman Declaration, COVID-19 had the doors firmly bolted. The only way to remember the founding moment of the EU was via blogs, Youtube videos and tweets from European decision makers. One blog that drew my attention was by the EU's high representative Josep Borrell. He gave a very personal account and drew to an ambitious close: 'As someone who has lived through European history with all its ups and downs, I am convinced we should think as

big and as creatively as Schuman – and act in that spirit.'
Think big and creatively. That's exactly what decision makers in some European capitals and institutions were doing in May. The realisation that this crisis could not be tackled with the usual rules and procedures had sunk in. The EU had to take a leap of faith, if not citizens would lose faith in the EU.

The first sign of a shift came on 15 May when the European Parliament asked for a €2 trillion European recovery instrument. It should be financed 'through the issuance of long-dated recovery bonds guaranteed by the EU budget'. So, back to borrowing again? Pretty much. The fact that the so-called 'recovery bonds' were supported by five of the six biggest groups in the European Parliament (all except the far-right) was unique. What was equally interesting: the parties in the European Parliament that formed the German coalition government, SPD and CDU, also supported it. Did this mean that Germany itself had finally come round?

The answer came three days later when president Macron and chancellor Merkel presented a French-German initiative on Europe's recovery from the coronacrisis. Germany and France joining forces to lead the European Union out of the crisis was in itself good news. Since 2012 many thought the Franco-German tandem had run out of steam. Germany's political and economic strength had become so dominant in Europe that it was like France was holding them back. On issues related to the euro, and by extension socio-economic policy, they barely saw eye to eye.

President Macron's election in 2017, won off the back of an ambitious and activist pro-European contest, definitely brought them closer together. But it was no 'Merkozy', as the close relationship between Merkel and the French president Sarkozy in 2011-2012 was called. They were not following in the footsteps of de Gaulle-Adenauer,

Pompidou-Brandt or Mitterrand-Kohl, whose picture of them holding hands at a World War I battlefield became iconic. But popular claims that we have reached the end of the Franco-German love-in, as *The Financial Times* wrote in April 2019 were exaggerated. The joint initiative of May 2020 showed that The Franco-German pair could kiss and make up when it needed to.

Even more remarkable than this united front was that Germany's position had changed dramatically, notably on the issue of financial solidarity. In the joint initiative both countries proposed the creation of a €500 billion recovery fund. The fund would be fuelled by joint debt: money that the European Commission would borrow on the market in the name of the EU. That money would then be distributed to regions and sectors most affected by the pandemic in the form of grants. For the very first time Merkel accepted, and even proposed, this way of working, after careful coordination with her social-democratic vice-chancellor Scholz. Right after, her CDU party welcomed the proposal as a major contribution to European solidarity in the corona crisis.

The die was cast. Several observers, keen to underline the historic importance of this turning point, went back to American history and called it Europe's 'Hamiltonian moment'. This was a reference to the first American Secretary of the Treasury, Alexander Hamilton, who in 1790 allowed the new US government to assume the debts incurred by the individual states during the War of Independence, thereby laying the foundation of a strong centralised federal government. Obviously, the European Union is not there (yet), and might never get there. But what is certain, is that with this decision, Merkel enters the European history books.

The Recovery Fund was not the only interesting proposal Merkel and Macron made that day, far from it. But the fact that a long-term German taboo had been shattered got most of the media attention. It made way for the recovery package that the Commission was asked to present. On 27 May, von der Leyen was ready for it.

EUROPE'S MOMENT

'This is Europe's moment. (…) We take that leap forward. We pave a strong path for our people and for the next generation.' With these words Commission president von der Leyen introduced her recovery package to the European Parliament. It was baptised: Next Generation EU. Big words are not uncommon in the EU. They accompany every new strategy, every new plan that is presented. But this time, there was also an air of big money in the room. And of big principles.

Next Generation EU is a solid fusion of three elements. First, the enhanced openness towards real financial solidarity that had grown over the course of the crisis and now had the backing of Paris and Berlin. Second, the lessons learned from the COVID-19 crisis. And third, the priorities that the new Commission had identified when it started work in 2019, notably the Green Deal and a Digital Europe.

At the core of this solidarity was a €750 billion recovery instrument, some kind of 'fund' to finance Europe's recovery. The fund was very much in line with the Franco-German initiative and the proposals of the European Parliament. For sure, it was smaller than what the European Parliament proposed and more than what the Franco-German initiative put on the table. But the basic idea was the same: the European Commission borrows the money from the market under very favourable conditions. Interest rates can be close to zero, because the EU's Multiannual Financial Framework (i.e. budget) is used as a guarantee. €250 billion would then be handed out in the form of cheap loans. But the larger chunk, €500 billion, would be distributed as grants (gifts) to countries that needed it most because they can't afford to get their economy back on track. Even though the hardest-hit countries, such as Spain and Italy, would be the main beneficiaries of the Fund, this was in the interests of all. Italy, for instance, was Germany's fifth largest trading partner and German machine producers relied heavily on suppliers from northern Italy. If Italy's economy did not pick up, Germany would be one of the first to feel the pinch. It could even undermine the eurozone as a whole. A factor that partially explains the German U-turn.

Over the thirty years 2028-2058, the €750 billion have to be repaid out of the EU budget which every EU country pays into. This is another element of solidarity. To reduce the burden on the countries even more, the Commission suggested introducing European taxes to try and raise some extra cash. Why not impose a tax on imported products with a high CO_2 footprint? Or on the major digital platforms? Or on big companies that reap the fruits the single market? If all these new sources of income are used to repay the borrowed money, countries would have to put less in themselves.

For the Commission, this proposal was a middle ground between northern and southern Europe. Unlike the ESM credit line agreed by the finance ministers on 9 April, this fund was mostly made up of grants, not just loans. Moreover, the strict conditionality that had accompanied the eurocrisis rescue packages, and that forced countries to take tough austerity measures, seemed to be a thing of the past. At the same time, the concerns of the northern countries were also being heard. This new fund had nothing to do with the debts of the past, as von der Leyen stressed in her speech to the Parliament. Countries that received support could not use it to repay their past debt.

They alone remained responsible for that. Countries like Germany would not become liable for another country's existing debt. It only covered *new* spending related to post-COVID recovery. Therefore, this was different from the eurobonds proposed during the eurocrisis. On top of that, the fund was a one-off and would expire once the last cent is repaid.

Next, the Commission also integrated some of the lessons learned from the COVID-19 crisis in its proposal. The recovery instrument should be first and foremost used to address the weaknesses that the pandemic had uncovered. There was money to strengthen Europe's strategic autonomy in key technologies; to extend the SURE program, which supported short-time work; to preserve the liquidity of small and medium enterprises; to launch a new €9.4 billion programme, EU4Health, to ensure the EU would not run out of vital medicines or medical equipment. 9.4 billion, that is 23 times the amount of the current programme.

To make even more money available to address the weaknesses that the pandemic had uncovered, the Commission also made some adjustments to its proposal for the Multiannual Financial Framework. For as long as the European Council had not found an agreement on this €1100 budget, changes were still possible. The Commission's suggestions ranged from increasing the budget for research and innovation in health to increasing the budget for the partners in the Western Balkan region.

A third and final important element in the Commission's proposal is that both in the €750 billion recovery instrument and in the adjusted €1100 billion Multiannual Financial Framework, the Commission did not weaken its commitment to its two main priorities: the Green Deal and Digital Europe. All investments made under Next Generation EU had to be green and digital. If not, Europe's economic recovery would not be sustainable, nor fit for the future. Investments in digital capacity, Artificial Intelligence, 5G and 6G, cybersecurity and supercomputers were strongly encouraged. As were investments in the renovation of buildings, which creates jobs and reduces energy bills. The time had come to launch a genuine renovation wave, Commission vice president Timmermans, in charge of the Green Deal, argued. In the transport sector, investments should be used first and foremost to make European cars and planes more sustainable, to give a boost to clean technologies such as clean hydrogen, and to finance 1 million electric-vehicle charging points. This is the kind of recovery the Commission put on the table. Timmermans summed it up as follows: 'We came to the conclusion that the risk of throwing money at the old economy of the 20th century is huge.' This had to be avoided at all costs, he warned.

Not everyone drew the same lessons from the pandemic, however. For some, the crisis created a 'let's not run before we can walk' sentiment. All green strategies better be put on hold. The Czech prime minister suggested to simply 'forget about' the Green Deal: it was 'too expensive'. But the Commission did not give in. To defend its position, the Commission repeatedly referred to an agreement reached by the European Council on 26 March. In that agreement the leaders explicitly mentioned the importance of the Green Deal in a post-COVID-19 Europe: 'We should start to prepare the measures necessary to get back to a normal functioning of our societies and economies and to sustainable growth, *integrating inter alia the green transition* and the digital transformation'. If a prime minister had 'forgotten' this, it sufficed to remind them that they were in the room when the text was approved.

On 21 July, less than two months after the European Commission had presented its proposals, the 27 leaders reached a landmark agreement on the EU's long-term budget and the shorter term recovery fund. The first physical meeting of the European Council after the crisis, in which the leaders could once again negotiate face to face, was a very difficult one. Four days and four nights, 90 hours, from Friday afternoon until Tuesday morning: that's the time they needed to overcome the strong differences in opinion amongst them.

In such negotiations, each prime minister or president has to be able to claim a victory, so the final, hard-fought compromise was not 100% what the Commission had proposed. Four so-called 'frugal' countries - Austria, Denmark, Sweden and especially the Netherlands - were strongly opposed to the very principle of the European Commission borrowing money on the capital markets on behalf of the Union, as Macron, Merkel and the Commission had proposed. As a compromise, the principle was accepted. However, within the €750 billion that the Commission could borrow, the amount of money that would be given - as grants that did not have to be repaid - to the countries hardest-hit by the COVID-19 crisis was reduced from €500 billion in the Commission proposal to €390. The rest - €360 billion - were loans.

The 'frugals' also wanted to have more of a view on how the beneficiary countries would use these grants, as well as guarantees that these countries were serious about modernising and reforming their economies. If they see insufficient progress, the money could be frozen, and the issue could be put on the agenda of the European Council, where every country de facto has a veto right. There were also a few other ways to sweeten the bitter pill the 'frugals' were having to swallow by accepting the joint borrowing: the overall EU budget was somewhat reduced, as were their contributions to it. To compensate for this loss of income, there were additional budget cuts in areas such as research and innovation, migration, humanitarian aid, health (!), digital Europe and assistance to regions that are moving out of the fossil-fuel era. Tough choices!

All countries having to agree in the European Council led to another outcome that was not ideal. The language on so-called 'rule of law' conditionality remained rather general. The moment the European Council meeting was over, the Hungarian and Polish leaders therefore ran to their press conference to claim that there was no link between getting EU funding and respecting the rule of law at all. Sooner or later - I hope sooner - this issue will come back on the European political agenda, starting with the European Parliament.

Solidarity is fragile. The temptation to put short-term national interests before longer-term 'enlightened self-interest' is huge. But all in all, the overall architecture of the Multiannual Financial Framework and Next Generation EU remained intact, including some first lessons drawn from the COVID-19 crisis. The creation of a recovery fund, financed through common debt, as well as the new sources of EU income that the leaders agreed are major steps forward. The decision that 30% of the entire EU budget will go to climate action, is equally crucial.

Therefore, the agreement was about more than just numbers, however important these were. On 21 July, the European Council agreed on a political project, a compass to get the Union safely through the new storm clouds that were already gathering on the horizon. This required fundamental choices, not an easy task with 27 partners around the table. But not reaching an agreement was never an option.

CHAPTER 16

Europe Reinvented

- How historians might look back at this pandemic
- What we still can learn from Machiavelli
- Why this book had to be written

The EU's journey through the COVID-19 crisis was a rollercoaster ride. Between January and July 2020, the mood swung from initial denial and self-confidence, to surprise and selfishness and finally to resilience, solidarity and resolve. Now that we have reached the end of this six-month journey, we can step back and ask two more fundamental questions: will the COVID-19 crisis lead to radical change in the way we live? And what lasting effect will it have on the European Union? The honest answer is: 'Let's see in one, five or ten years'. But that doesn't help us get back on our feet much. The least I can offer are some personal reflections, fully aware that until a vaccine is found, the situation will remain precarious, possibly with a second wave in parts of the European continent.

BEFORE CORONA, AFTER CORONA

Will our lives be radically different before and after the corona crisis? Will there be a 'BC and AC', a 'Before Corona and After Corona'? In a broader historical context: no. This may come as a surprise. But there is no comparison with for instance the bacterium (not a virus) that caused the Black Death. This disease, which peaked in 1347-1351 and killed around half of the European population, did drastically change the course of European history. It had a huge socio-economic impact and changed world views to such an extent that it led to a whole new cultural era, the Renaissance. According to some historians the Black Death had such a major environmental impact that it even caused the Little Ice Age.

Nor will COVID-19 have the same disruptive impact as the sequence of events between 1914 and 1945 – World War I, the Great Depression and World War II – which resulted in a radically new and different world order and, in Western Europe, to the modern welfare state. Read Tony Judt's *Postwar: A History of Europe since 1945*. After World War II 20% (in France) and 40% (in Germany) of houses were destroyed. Transport infrastructure was destroyed. Much of the economic infrastructure was destroyed. Famine and shortages of all kinds were a reality. After the pandemic hit Europe, the infrastructure is still intact. And institutions that sustain the global order, such as the United Nations, the International Monetary Fund and the World Bank, are still around, even though they have had a rough ride.

The reason why there will not be a new BC and AC is that we have moved on. We are already much more capable of cushioning the impact of the pandemic. We don't have a vaccine (yet), but at least in Europe we have well-trained doctors and nurses as well as the medical equipment to curb the mortality rate. As for the economic impact, we now have a wealth of tools and economic models, fine-tuned since the 2008-2010 economic crisis, to take faster and more efficient action. During the Great Depression, it took several years before a recovery package was put together. It was only then that the modern concept of Gross Domestic Product was developed, by Simon Kuznets in 1934. This time around, governments and central banks intervened within weeks. History helps put things in perspective.

From a short-term perspective, however, the impact of the pandemic is obviously huge. Many people lost their job, their company or even worse, their life or their loved-ones. On a positive note, in many areas the impossible suddenly became possible. Lengthy discussions on teleworking, long-distance teaching and the pro and cons of videoconferencing were cut short: all these new ways of working were implemented in record time, on a scale never seen before. In big cities, traffic jams disappeared and air quality improved considerably. Lockdowns killed FOMO – the Fear of Missing Out – and people rediscovered the joy of slowing down. There were many warm shows of solidarity such as restaurant owners bringing food to medical staff at the hospital next-door and prison inmates voluntarily producing face masks. For some, the hyper-individualism of the neoliberal period was on its way out, bowing out to a stronger sense of community and collectivity. Gardening, cooking and urban farming became more popular and the value of local food products was rediscovered. Awareness of the importance of personal hygiene, especially washing your hands, increased. And e-commerce kept at least some businesses going.

But there was also a downside to the measures. The lockdowns aggravated the inequalities within society. Self-isolating in a spacious house with a garden and a private pool is very different than in a studio apartment with no balcony. With the local playground closed, children growing up in a house without a garden cannot play outside and breathe fresh air. The lockdown also put a question mark over creating more housing in cities, as urban planners had been promoting. When access to public space is restricted, it's far better to live in the countryside than in an apartment block in the city. While we're on the topic of green living: the use of plastic bags and single use plastic increased again. In a few cases environmentally friendly reusable cups were banned. The lockdown also led to an increase in domestic violence, loneliness and bore-outs. Burn-outs lurked around the corner for overworked medical staff and parents juggling homeworking and childcare. Teleworking is great in theory, but impossible for sixty percent of workers due to the nature of their job, creating yet more new inequalities. Long-distance learning widened the gap between families with a computer and internet and those without. It started to dawn on many that the future would not necessarily be brighter but, on the contrary, full of risks.

Not all of these changes will last. Routines are remarkably persistent. Is it too pessimistic to assume that, without additional measures, traffic jams will soon be back, people will start travelling again and CO2 emissions will increase dramatically? Probably not. But some of these changes will stick around post-COVID-19, for better or worse. There will probably be more e-commerce, teleworking, videoconferencing and long-distance teaching. But there will also be more psychological problems, higher social inequality, and students lagging behind.

Supporting the positive changes ('never waste a good crisis') and tackling the negative ones requires policy. The choices that are made now will determine the next decade. Some of these decisions will be taken at the local or (sub)national level. But crucial decisions on our post-COVID societies and economies will be taken at the European level. Hence the second question: what lasting effect will it have on the EU? Will it come out of the crisis weaker or stronger?

EUROPE REINVENTED

To reinvent means to build something new based on what already exists. In the case of the EU the basis to build on is there. The Lisbon Treaty, which sets out how the EU functions, came into force just over a decade ago. Roughly the same number of countries (Croatia joined in 2013, the UK left in 2020) have got used to working together within that rather stable architecture. Since then the EU also went through a series of crises, notably the eurocrisis and the migration crisis. Each one left its mark and added new tools to the EU crisis management toolbox. But as shown in previous chapters, the COVID-19 pandemic will have an even greater impact than previous crises.

Let me highlight five elements that together sow the seeds of a stronger European Union. A Union that will take its place in the world with its own model, alongside the American and Chinese models.

First, the pandemic is the perfect excuse to strengthen the eurozone and finally complete it. In acute crises the European Central Bank is crucial to push more money into an ailing economy. Between 12 March and 4 May 2020 alone, the bank decided to buy bonds worth €1470 billion, an enormous amount, almost seven times the effort they made to save the euro in 2010-2012. Back then, this bond-buying activity and the very low interest rates set by the ECB were supposed to be temporary measures. But they were never really dismantled. Governments have become used, even addicted, to the cheap money of the ECB.

This is not sustainable long-term. When money is cheap it easily ends up in the hands of 'zombie-companies' that survive on cheap credit but don't really boost the real economy. It can also create economic bubbles. More importantly, simply hiding or transferring national debt to the ECB cannot go on forever. Sooner or later, the bill will arrive. On 5 May the German Constitutional Court argued in a landmark judgement – and I simplify the decision here – that the ECB did not correctly justify its government bond buying programme. By early July, Germany and the ECB had found a smooth way out, so that Germany can remain part of the programme. But more structurally, the eurozone's continued dependency on the ECB and the long-term risks of buying more and more government debt require a more solid answer. If the eurozone would have its own budget to support countries or certain economic sectors in times of crisis, then it would be less dependent on the ECB.

The recovery instrument proposed by the European Commission as part of its Next Generation Europe proposal is a step in that direction. A European Union that uses its own budget to borrow money on the market, then gives part of that money as grants to countries in need and feeds its budget through new European taxes, is a significant shift for the EU. If this is complemented by the Banking and the Capital Market Unions being up and running, the eurozone would be much better equipped to handle the economic storms on the horizon. It would change the eurozone in a way that before (and without) the COVID-19 pandemic would have been unthinkable.

Economic recovery will only take place under certain conditions. This brings me to the second impact element of the COVID-19 crisis: the changing role of the state. After four decades of the neo-liberal motto 'private good, public bad', the state is back in fashion. The economic crisis, in which governments had to save the banks, was the door starting to edge open. But COVID-19 has taken it completely off its hinges. In the post-COVID recovery period, a stronger state will be indispensable. Tough decisions have to be made on how to distribute investments to get the economy back on track: to the economy, social policy, the environment, healthcare, culture, and that's just for starters. It is only the state that can take such decisions at the national level.

Here, some caveats apply. The more interventionalist state needed in times of a real crisis is not always without risk. Too much regulation, too much intervention strangles innovation and entrepreneurship, both essential to lift Europe out of this crisis. Time to dust off your 2013 copy of Mariana Mazzucato's *The Entrepreneurial State*! Governments also tend to listen just a bit better to bigger companies, at the expense of smaller entrepreneurs with less access to the state apparatus. And at the expense of free competition, which is crucial for hard-hit consumers.

Therefore, although national governments are in charge, a strict European framework is indispensable. First of all, this implies a return to the state aid rules, which were suspended during the COVID-19 crisis. If this does not happen, recovery could be a very bumpy ride. This widens the economic gap between different countries and undermines the eurozone. Second, and for the same reason, it requires the reanimation of the Stability and Growth Pact, the second set of rules that was put on hold during the crisis. Third, it requires the full restoration of the single market and the Schengen Area, a prerequisite for a speedy recovery. And fourth, it requires coordination on which strategic sectors to invest in, such as the green energy, digital and innovation. If not, recovery will be fragmented according to national preferences. Or slowed down when governments feel forced, for domestic reasons, to invest in the sectors of the past. New Generation Europe gives the direction on where investments should flow to, but not much more. This should be addressed. The recovery will be European, or it will not be at all.

The third impact area that became very visible during the crisis was the need for more strategic autonomy or economic sovereignty. Much was said about this in chapter thirteen. Let me give one more example: Europe's digital sovereignty. The future is digital. The EU should not become the assembly line for the hardware of American and Chinese software. The decision taken by France and Germany on 4 May to create a European cloud space, located in Brussels as of early 2021, is a big step forward. Right now, European companies depend on one of the four players that dominate the market: American Google, AWS and Microsoft and Chinese Alibaba. With this new initiative, named Gaia-X, European companies can now store and exchange data in the European cloud, according to European norms and standards. Another illustration of how the EU is reinventing itself.

The fourth area of impact is Europe's soft power. During three long months, between March and May, Europe was the epicentre of the COVID outbreak. This had a negative impact on Europe's image. The lack of solidarity, both with other EU countries and neighbouring countries, was a grave mistake. During the crisis this was fully exploited by countries like China, eager to increase its own soft power. But the pandemic also offers opportunities. Throughout the crisis, European leaders demonstrated how much importance they attach to saving the lives of European citizens, despite the huge impact on the economy. Protecting its citizens is part and parcel of the European social contract, ever since John Locke published his Two Treatises, in 1689. Other fundamental rights are equally part of Europe's DNA. A strong attachment to privacy rights, for instance, set Europe apart from several Asian countries which used rather invasive methods to curb the epidemic. And the international leadership role the European Union assumed, by hosting a major donor conference or by setting up a humanitarian air bridge with mainly Africa, shows that the EU can be counted on. Here again, one important caveat: there are no circumstances under which the EU is prepared to compromise on the rule of law, human rights and democracy. While the COVID-19 crisis led to an increase of stronger governmental or even authoritarian power, the EU should remain a beacon of democratic values. It will pay off.

Finally, and fifthly, the pandemic showed the importance of foresight and emergency preparedness. This is not new. More than 500 years ago, Niccolò Machiavelli wrote appropriately: '[a disease] in the commencement is easy to cure and difficult to understand; but when it has neither been discovered in time nor treated upon a proper principle, it becomes easy to understand and difficult to cure. The same thing happens in state affairs; by foreseeing them at a distance (…) the evils which might arise from them are soon cured; but when, from want of foresight, they are suffered to increase to such a degree they are perceptible to everyone, there is no longer a remedy.' In other words, what goes for a disease like COVID-19 also goes for policy-making. Yet, as this outbreak made clear, the information is often known, but not sufficiently integrated in policy or policy planning, as the second chapter showed. The EU now has a commissioner in charge of foresight, the External Action Service has a Policy Planning Unit, several national foreign ministries increasingly invest in foresight. It is time to bring all this work together and integrate it much deeper in daily decision-making. This, together with stronger crisis response tools, will put the EU in a position to shape rather than undergo future crises.

In the coming months and years there will be no shortage of future crises, on top of the fall-out of the COVID outbreak. The threat of illegal migration is still there. Throughout the COVID crisis, the pressure on the Eastern Mediterranean Route and the Central Mediterranean Route increased. Armed conflict in Europe's neighbourhood has not diminished and might further increase while the world's focus is elsewhere. Inequality will increase worldwide. Populism, though not very vocal during the crisis, will raise its head again, fully exploiting the socio-economic difficulties caused by the pandemic. And the next deadly virus is just biding its time. Perhaps next time it will be a Nipah or Hendra. Whatever it is, it will come.

But the biggest challenge of all is already right in front of our noses. It is linked to all the other challenges I just mentioned, from migration and armed conflict to rising inequality and the outbreak of a new epidemic: climate change. This pandemic showed the importance of science. In every European country virologists were raised to celebrity or even hero status, and quite rightly so. They were the first thing we heard in the morning, and the last thing we heard before bed. It's time we listen with the same intensity to climate science and climate scientists. In COVID times, we focused on the cavalry scout. Now it's time to focus with even more intensity on the cavalry. In this area the EU does not have to reinvent itself. It is already the world's climate leader in an increasingly leaderless world *and* it has the right toolbox: the European Green Deal. It's just a matter of rolling it out, as part of a reinvented Europe.

On 7 April, the much-respected American scholar Richard Haass wrote a *Foreign Affairs* article with the title *The Pandemic Will Accelerate History Rather Than Reshape It*. The article influenced several parts of this book. Except one paragraph in his article: 'The spread of COVID19 to and through Europe has also highlighted the loss of momentum of the European project. (...) The process of European integration had run out of steam long before this crisis – as Brexit demonstrated especially clearly. The principal question in the post-pandemic world is how much the pendulum will continue to swing from Brussels to national capitals.' I started writing this book on 8 April. I hope it provides an answer to that question.

AFTERWORD BY JEREMY RIFKIN

We should have known. The warning signs and alarm bells were going off for more than a decade, but the world was asleep. The COVID-19 virus was inevitable, but we chose to close our eyes, and now we have to cover our mouths with masks. We have witnessed an escalating number of global pandemics over the past decades – SARS, Ebola, Zika, Swine flu, HIV – with increasing virulence and impacts on global public health, and now COVID-19.

The escalation in global pandemics is not a coincidence or just bad luck. These pandemics are intimately connected to modern economic development and a fossil fuel-based civilization. A century ago, the wild still made up 75% of the Earth's landmass. Today, less than 23% of the world is categorized as wild. The reason is that the rise in the human population from 1.8 billion people in 1920 to more than 7 billion people in 2020 was made possible by the conversion of the wild to agricultural production as well as urban and industrial development. Humanity is now expropriating the equivalent of one and a half earths to maintain a growing population in a globalized economy. As the wilderness diminishes, human populations are coming closer and closer to the Earth's remaining wild species and the viruses that inhabit them.

At the same time, the emission of global warming gasses from burning fossil fuels has resulted in the rise of the Earth's temperature, forcing a change in the planet's hydrological cycle. For every one degree Celsius that the temperature goes up on Earth due to global warming emissions, the atmosphere is absorbing 7% more precipitation from the ground, which results in more concentrated precipitation in the clouds, and more extreme unpredictable water events – blockbuster winter snows, massive spring floods, extensive summer droughts and wildfires, and powerful hurricanes – that are devastating ecosystems around the world. Our ecosystems cannot catch up to the exponential shift in the Earth's hydrological cycle and are collapsing in real time, forcing mass migrations, not only of our own species but also all the other species on Earth. Viruses are hitching a ride on our fellow species and coming into more frequent contact with human populations, creating escalating pandemic outbreaks.

The long and short of it is that all species on Earth are becoming climate refugees and we have not yet fully comprehended the consequences. What we are discovering, in real time, is that changes to any one of the Earth's spheres – atmosphere, biosphere, lithosphere, hydrosphere – spill over and affect every other sphere and, not surprising, every species, including our own.

In reality, what each of us does in our everyday lives intimately affects everything else on Earth and comes back to affect us as well. We are learning that there are no real boundaries in nature. We will either all come together to protect our common biosphere, or pay a heavy price.

Where do we go from here? Peter Van Kemseke has provided a dramatic day-to-day nuanced account of the unfolding COVID-19 viral pandemic in the European Union and around the world. The story he tells is riveting but, even more important, it provides a frame of reference from which we can begin to entertain a new vision and narrative for the European Union and humanity, perhaps in time to mitigate the worst-case climate change scenarios that could take us over a red line and deep into the sixth extinction event of life on Earth.

Europe Reinvented serves as both a warning and a prescription of where we need to head now in the European Union – all of us – to ready ourselves for a new approach to life in our communities and on our continent. To this end, Peter is well positioned to help us navigate our way through the journey ahead. I have been fortunate to work closely with him for the past five years as an advisor to vice president Maroš Šefčovič who, at the time, was in charge of the Energy Union and Smart Europe and who is now in President Ursula von der Leyen's Commission serving as the vice president for Interinstitutional Relations and Long-Term Foresight and Policy.

Our joint work for vice president Šefčovič over the past half-decade focused on conceptualizing and deploying a smart digital infrastructure and a wholesale transition out of fossil fuels and into solar, wind, and other renewable energies that propel us into a post-carbon Third Industrial Revolution in the next stage of the European journey.

Every major economic infrastructure transformation in world history has required three elements, each of which interacts with the others to enable the system to operate as a whole: a new communication medium; a new power source; and a new transportation mechanism to 'manage', 'power', and 'move' society. Infrastructure paradigms also create new kinds of human habitats and are accompanied by new economic systems and new forms of governance to manage them. Although it's long been assumed that economic systems and forms of governance establish infrastructure, it is, rather, new infrastructure paradigms that largely determine the kinds of economic systems that plug into them and the forms of governance that oversee them.

Infrastructures, at the deepest level, represent an extension of what every organism needs to stay alive. Every organism needs a means to communicate, a continuous supply of energy to stay alive, a means of motility and mobility to engage its environment, and a semi-permeable membrane – a skin or shell – to mediate its internal life with the outside world. Infrastructures perform the same function. They allow ever-larger collectivities of human beings to engage in more complex, integrated, and inclusive economic, social, and political life as an extended social organism.

In the nineteenth century, steam-powered printing and the telegraph, abundant coal, and locomotives on national rail systems meshed in a common infrastructure to manage, power, and move society, giving birth to the First Industrial Revolution and the rise of urban habitats, capitalist economies, and national markets overseen by nation-state governance. In the twentieth century, centralized electricity, the telephone, radio and television, cheap oil, and internal combustion vehicles on national road systems converged to create an infrastructure for the Second Industrial Revolution and the rise of suburban habitats, globalization, and global governing institutions.

Now, we are on the cusp of a Third Industrial Revolution. The digitized broadband Communication Internet is converging with a digitized Continental Electricity Internet, powered by solar and wind electricity, and a digitized Mobility and Logistics Internet made up of autonomous electric and fuel-cell vehicles, powered from the electricity internet. These three internets are continuously being fed data from sensors embedded across society that are monitoring activity of all kinds in real time, from ecosystems, agricultural fields, warehouses, road systems, factory production lines, retail stores, and especially from the residential, commercial, and institutional building stock, allowing humanity to more efficiently manage, power, and move day-to-day economic activity and social life from where they work and live. This is the Internet of Things (IoT). In the coming era, buildings will be retrofitted for energy efficiency and climate resilience and embedded with IoT infrastructure. They will also be equipped with edge data centers, giving the public direct control over how their data is collected, used, and shared. Smart buildings will also serve as green micro power-generating plants, energy storage sites, and transport and logistics hubs for electric and fuel cell vehicles in a more distributed zero-emission society. Buildings in the Third Industrial Revolution will no longer be passive, walled-off private spaces but, rather, potentially actively engaged nodal entities sharing their renewable energies, energy efficiencies, energy storage, electric mobility, and a wide range of other economic and social activity with one another at the discretion of their occupants. Self-reliant, smart buildings are an essential component of the emerging Resilient Society.

I have no doubt that the academic community, government leaders, the business community, and a younger generation across the European Union, will benefit immensely from the analysis of how the European Union has approached the unfolding coronavirus pandemic crisis. Even more important, this book makes clear that an economic recovery from the greatest economic crisis in our lifetime will fail if the European Union and the European citizenry slip back and take the easy route by bailing out the very industries and business models that have caused the climate crisis and given rise to ever more dangerous viral pandemics. Instead, it stresses that Europe must reinvent itself by envisioning and deploying a smart, digital, zero-emission Third Industrial Revolution infrastructure and accompanying economic and social paradigm that can create a more resilient Europe and a more sustainable world. The von der Leyen Commission is steadfastly resolved to take the new route, and is calling upon every region in Europe and the citizens of the European Union to come together around the agenda of establishing a seamless and integrated European Union that can usher in a New Green Deal for current generations and those yet to come.

ACKNOWLEDGEMENTS

This is a book that wrote itself. It took shape page by page, as developments unfolded. *Europe Reinvented* is probably the first book written on how the European Union dealt with the worst crisis that hit the European continent and the world since World War II. Hopefully, in the near future, many more studies will follow. In-depth studies with footnotes and references to academic publications. Studies written with some more distance, after the dust has settled.

This is a different book. Perhaps a somewhat impatient book, but for sure a book that couldn't wait. Later in 2020, the European Union will launch the Conference on the Future of Europe, an opportunity for European citizens to claim their seat at the table. A chance to share their ideas and concerns. After all, the European Union will not only be reinvented by its institutions. It will be permanently reinvented by its citizens. By bringing some structure to the seemingly chaotic events that shook Europe in the first seven months of 2020, I hope my book can contribute to a well-informed discussion on what is at stake.

Europe Reinvented is therefore not written for experts in European affairs or for like-minded Europeans who already now embrace the European project (I would of course be very interested in their critical comments!). Its ambition is to reach out to anyone who is not very familiar with how the EU works; to politicians – even of mainstream parties – who still argue that the European Union was invisible in this crisis; to students who want a crash course in who does what in the EU; to anyone who tries to understand the Union but has a hard time understanding 'euro-jargon'. I warmly thank Heather Sills, Peter Schoenaerts and Wim Troch for their merciless hunt for such jargon. Even terms such as 'Member States' did not get past them. I am very grateful to them.

An accessible style should go hand in hand with accuracy. I am very grateful to a panel of excellent proofreaders who, despite their busy schedules, took time to read the manuscript, share their comments or expressed their support: Prof. dr. Herman Goossens (Antwerp University), Adalbert Jahnz (European Commission), José Leandro (European Bank for Reconstruction and Development), Peter Moors (secretary-general Belgian Foreign Ministry), Sarah Nelen (European Commission), Manuel Szapiro (European Commission; College of Europe), Didier Seeuws (Council of the European Union), Willem van de Voorde (Belgian ambassador to the EU), Wilfried Verachtert (IMEC) and Prof. dr. Hendrik Vos (Ghent University). Their insights improved the book beyond imagination. They can, of course, not be blamed for any mistakes in the final text.

Last but not least, a special thanks to professor and – if I may – my friend Jeremy Rifkin, who without any hesitation agreed to write the afterword. Through our many conversations he convinced me that international politics is not only about Realpolitik and geopolitics. It is also about vision and foresight. But perhaps also about dreaming of a better planet.

Peter Van Kemseke, 21 July 2020

Comments on the book? Please leave your reaction on **Peter Van Kemseke's LinkedIn page.**

ABOUT THE AUTHOR

Peter Van Kemseke holds a PhD in contemporary history and specialises in international relations. He studied in Leuven (Belgium), Hull (UK) and Los Angeles (US). As a Belgian diplomat he served at the OSCE, NATO, the United Nations in New York and the EU. He was deputy head of cabinet of European Council president Herman Van Rompuy and worked for European Commission vice-president Maroš Šefčovič. He has published books on diplomacy and European and global politics. His academic experience includes teaching at the European Studies programme of Leuven University. He is a frequent speaker on foreign policy and international relations.

'In all of our time together, Peter's patience, compassion, and unswerving commitment to helping the European Union and its citizenry prepare a more sustainable roadmap to heal the planet, while ensuring that all of its people have a say in their future and the future of their families, shone forth in every meeting and conversation. He made me realize that the real mark of a public servant is a deep-seated empathic sensibility that is always hopeful but never naïve. Peter believes that if given the chance and an even playing field, human beings, for the most part, will exhibit the best of our humanity and reach out to each other – and hopefully our fellow creatures – and make the world a better place for life to flourish.'

Jeremy Rifkin

COVID-19 TIMELINE:
25 KEY DATES

2019

December

31 China reports first 'pneumonia' case to WHO

2020

January

24 first known confirmed case in Europe (France)
27 first time mention of Coronavirus in an EU meeting
31 WHO declares Coronavirus a global health emergency

February

7 first discussion on Coronavirus by ministers in an EU meeting

24 rapid increase in confirmed COVID-19 cases in Italy

28 Italy formally asks the EU for help - no response

March

3-4 France and Germany restrict export of medical protective equipment

10 first discussion by European leaders in the European Council
11 WHO declares COVID-19 a pandemic
11 Schengen countries begin to introduce border restrictions
11 US suspends travel from Europe to the United States

15 EU restricts export of medical equipment outside of the EU

17 EU adopts temporary restrictions on non-essential travel to the EU
18 ECB announces the Pandemic Emergency Purchase Programme

23 Finance Ministers suspend Stability and Growth Pact obligations

2020

April

9 Finance Ministers agree on €540 billion support package

May

4 EU hosts Coronavirus Global Response pledging conference

8 first flight of the EU Humanitarian Air Bridge takes off

18 Macron and Merkel propose €500 billion EU recovery fund

27 European Commission presents 'Next Generation EU'
29 Latvia first EU country to launch a contact tracing app

June

1 borders gradually start to reopen in Schengen area

30 EU reopens external borders for a number of third countries

July

21 European Council approves EU multiyear budget and recovery package

CPSIA information can be obtained
at www.ICGtesting.com
Printed in the USA
LVHW030240270121
677549LV00011B/2064